CONTENTS

STANDARD TREASURY OF LEARNING

with

Funk & Wagnalls
DICTIONARY
For Young People

VOLUME FIVE

STANDARD REFERENCE WORKS PUBLISHING COMPANY, INC.

NEW YORK

HORSES

Illustrated by E. Joseph Dreany

American Saddle Horse

For smooth riding, horsemen agree, there's no horse like the American Saddle Horse. Built for comfort, this graceful animal seems to "float through the air with the greatest of ease." This accounts for his popularity among people whose hobby is horseback riding.

Plantation owners in the old South used to travel miles inspecting their fields. They needed a gentle, steady mount, and found these qualities in a horse descended from English stock. The American Saddle Horse of today is descended from a cross of these plantation horses and a breed called the Thoroughbred.

Appaloosa

Most spots can be washed off. Neither soap and water nor dry cleaning will change the Appaloosa, for this horse's mottled blue spots are there to stay. They give a most curious look to this grey, bay, chestnut or cream-colored animal — almost as if some one had waved a dripping paintbrush over his back.

This peculiarly marked pony was bred in western Indian country. Certain Indian tribes had large herds of Appaloosa and these horses were ideal for ranch work.

Out West the Appaloosa is still a favorite ranch horse and he is liked for his speed, endurance and intelligence.

Arabian

A man will often let his dog sleep at the foot of his bed, but his horse usually sleeps outside in the stable. On the Arabian desert, however, it was not unusual in days gone by for an Arabian horse to sleep in his master's tent. Tribal warfare often put the Arab in danger of attack. At the slightest noise outside the tent the horse would rise and prepare to defend his sleeping master.

Loyalty, bravery, speed and great endurance without food or water gave fame to the Arabian horse. Beauty, too, distinguishes this noble animal. His lines are clean-cut, his ears curved and pointed, and above his well-formed nose is a small dent known as a "dish."

Taken from Arabia across Africa to Spain, the Arabian horse was brought to America in the 16th century. Today almost every light-weight American horse has some Arabian blood.

Bronco

"Ride him cowboy! Hold your seat!" A tall order for the bronco buster at a rodeo. If he can keep his seat until the whistle blows — holding a rope with only one hand — the cowboy has a fair chance at a prize. But the horse he rides was chosen especially for his mean, uncontrollable temper. Bronco, which comes from the Spanish word meaning "wild," is applied to any horse who shows a vicious defiance and a refusal to be saddle broken.

Out West the cowboys tackle these unmanageable horses for the fun of proving their horsemanship. The sport has proved so exciting that throughout the country, even in New York City's tremendous Madison Square Garden, people pay admission to the rodeo — where the bucking bronco thrills the crowd and spills many a cowboy.

Clydesdale

Tommy is a farm boy. He can hardly remember when he first began to do his share of the farm work. Relaxing on his fine draft horse at the end of a hard day's work behind the plow, he waits while his thirsty friend takes a big drink of water.

Tommy's horse is a Clydesdale — named after the river Clyde in Scotland. The Clydesdale was brought to this country to help the farmer work his fields, to pull the farmer's wagons and sleighs. He is easily broken to harness and can pull a fairly heavy load with ease. Tommy's horse has white markings on his face and white "stockings" on his legs — like so many horses which belong to this handsome and hard-working breed.

Percheron

On the very same farm we see Tommy's father leading another horse to pasture. This animal, a Percheron, belongs to the breed which carried the knights of old on their long Crusades. Joan of Arc rode a Percheron when she led the French armies against the English.

The Percheron is named after a district in France known as "Le Perche," where these fine, sturdy horses originated. Percherons were originally brought over to the United States in the early 1800's and during the Civil War were used extensively for army draft work.

Years ago, before we had motor-driven trucks, this type of horse could be seen hauling a clumsy milk wagon along the streets. Today the Percheron is used for heavy farm work. Despite his life of toil, this horse has a beauty of form which often earns him prizes. Last year Tommy's father took two of his Percherons to the State Fair, and won a ribbon for the best-matched team in the show.

Fire Horse

Fire! Fire! Today when the alarm sounds the firemen jump into position on their long, red, motor-driven trucks and away they go!

In grandfather's day things were quite different. Horses took the place of a motor. Three galloping horses could be seen dashing through the streets at the head of the old brass fire engine. Clouds of smoke poured through the funnel as the horses pulled away at the harness, speeding to reach the fire in time. Bells rang out to warn all passers-by.

It was hard work for both the firemen and their horses. Between alarms the horses rested quietly in the fire hall. But when the alarm sounded, things began to happen! Down the pole slid the firemen — the harnesses, suspended lightly overhead, were dropped onto the

horses' backs — with a great clanging of bells they went speeding off to fight the fire!

Fire horses were not all of the same breed, but generally they were of the Percheron type. They had to be strong, powerful horses. They had to have courage and be obedient. To pull the heavy wagon, to stand at attention while the firemen worked, to follow the slightest tug at the reins, these were just a few of the fire horse's duties.

The use of these horses was discontinued in the early part of this century when they were replaced by motorized equipment. These picturesque horses were shifted to farm and country where they lived long and useful lives.

Hackney

"Fetch the carriage, James!" No one says that these days, for we ride by bus, by automobile, by train and by plane. There was a time when the carriage would be rolled out with two sturdy, heavy horses at its head. These carriage horses were called Hackneys.

High stepping, elegant and striking, Hackneys are the pride of the show ring today. The Hackney can be a bit rough for saddle riding, as the high-prancing action, so stirring to watch, is sometimes tiring to a rider.

Harness Horse

"My horse can kick the dust in your horse's face," said one farmer to another as they passed each other on a country road. Both were driving their iron-wheeled rigs to town, the day was sunny and bright, the mood was right for a friendly race. That is how harness racing first began. Today it is a well-known sport, carefully regulated by rules and accepted customs.

At a harness race nowadays you will see the Standard Bred (the breed of horse generally used) speeding with determination and control around the track at the head of a sulky. The sulky, a two-wheeled cart, rides on air-filled rubber tires — a great improvement over the heavy old iron wheels. The driver wears a gayly colored cap and jacket, the sulky wheels spin faster and faster, and the crowd cheers as the horses race around the track.

Indian Cayuse

Before the coming of the White Man, the American Indians traveled on foot and located their small villages near the best supply of game. When food became scarce they packed up their few possessions and moved on. As the wild horses appeared on the prairies, the Comanches and other tribes captured and tamed them.

Mounted on these fierce, wild ponies they were able to pursue the huge herds of buffalo which roamed the Western Plains. The Indians were great horse traders, too. Sometimes a band of painted Redmen would swoop down on a band of domestic animals and drive them off into the wilderness.

An Indian afoot on the plains or prairie was in a very bad situation. Good horsemanship soon became one of the chief virtues and an Indian child learned to ride almost as early as it learned to walk. The Indians usually rode without a saddle, unless they were near a white settlement where saddles could be obtained.

The Cayuse pony is named after a tribe of western American Indians, and is descended from the Spanish horses brought over by Cortes. While the Cayuse is still to be found on Indian Reservations, it is no longer depended on and is today just a type of western horse.

The small picture below shows a spotted horse known as a Pinto, a name taken from the Spanish word meaning "paint" The scene is that of an early American Indian carting bundles placed on two long poles. This was in the days before wheels were known to them.

Morgan

A man once loved a horse so much that he named it after himself. This man was Justin Morgan, who moved to Vermont in 1795 bringing with him his horse, Justin Morgan. Most people have never heard of the man, but the horse and all the Morgan horses which came after it are known throughout America.

This first Morgan horse was small, but unbelievably strong and fast. Used for saddle or carriage riding, for weight pulling, for farm work, this horse showed unflagging determination to do the job well.

He lived twenty-nine years — a long life for a horse. Morgan horses of the present day are used mainly in farming, but there are still Morgans to be seen on the race tracks.

Mule

He looks like a horse, yet he doesn't look like a horse. Is this a riddle? No, it's a mule — produced by the mating of a donkey with a mare horse. His long ears and odd voice make him quite different from a horse. Different, but just as useful.

In the early days of the West mules carried loads through the hot, dry deserts and over steep mountain paths. Mule trains hauled borax in heavy wagons across Death Valley. The sure-footed mule seldom slipped on the roughest mountain roads, his willing spirit tackled the hardest of jobs.

A mule can do the same work as a horse — bearing loads on his back, traveling up and down hills with a saddle and rider, trudging along the road at the head of a farmer's hay wagon — and he can do this work with less care and less food than a horse.

Mustang

Not all stray Spanish Horses were captured by the Indians. Some wandered about confused and frightened by their newly won independence. Like men, they organized into little societies for protection against wolves and other wild animals. In what might almost be called elections, these wild horses, or Mustangs, chose their leaders.

The elections were not a matter of dropping ballots into a box, but of fighting for the leadership with flying hoofs, bared teeth and wild snorts. The job fell to the fiercest, who in turn was driven from the "presidency" in his old age by a younger, stronger horse.

Tales of these Mustang bands led cowboys, in later days, to ride out in groups with the object of capturing and training some horses. This may seem like a cheap way to get a horse, but the hard work involved more than equaled the value of the horse. Riding miles from the home ranch, the cowboys would finally spot a body of Mustangs up in the hills or in some hard-to-find valley. Their task was to drive the horses into a canyon, block up one end of the canyon and then rope one horse at a time. Gradually, cowboys trained these wild horses to work on the ranches.

Palomino

"I love a parade!" Could it have been a Palomino who first spoke these words? There are few sights as pretty as this golden horse prancing along at the head of a parade, waving his white mane and holding his tail high and proud.

Yes, the Palomino is a favorite parade horse, but he is a hard worker too. On the ranch some of his duties are rounding up cattle, riding over the range in search of a lost steer, carrying his master on visits from ranch to ranch.

Palominos are not yet a distinct breed, any horse of this special creamy color and marking fits the title. The Palomino seems somehow to realize his beauty and when chosen to make movies will strut gaily before the cameras.

Circus Horse

The circus is coming to town! You will see the swaggering clowns and the squealing calliope, the fierce old lion and the laughing fat lady, pink cotton candy, the clumsy elephant and the beautiful white circus horse. Beauty and brains are what the circus horse needs. It doesn't matter much what type he is — a Percheron, a western horse, a Palomino or a pony. He must be a natural showman.

The heavier variety of horse is used for bareback riding because he has a flat, broad back. When these horses canter around the circus ring they do so evenly and smoothly, and this is very important to the performer. These horses are nearly always white.

Up and around goes the clown in a perfect somersault to land on the horse's back. This looks easy, but it calls for perfect timing. A careless horse would never do, his master might land on the hard ground.

Circus horses can be trained to do an endless number of tricks — standing straight and tall on their hind legs, waltzing about in time to music, bowing to the audience and even shaking hands with the ringmaster. And when the circus packs up and moves on, you may see at the head of the parade a strutting, prancing circus horse.

Pony Express

Mailing a letter is the easiest thing in the world. Put it in an envelope, seal the flap, paste down the stamp, drop it in the mailbox. Off it goes by train or plane, to be delivered by the postman a few days later.

A little less than one hundred years ago — before the railroad ran further West than Missouri — letters were carried from Missouri to the gold miners of California by Pony Express. The fastest horses and the best riders were chosen for this important task. Slinging a mailbag across the saddle, the rider mounted his horse and rode away at top speed. About ten miles from where he started, the Pony Express man would reach a way-station. There a fresh horse — all saddled and ready — stood waiting. Again the mailbag was slung across the saddle, the

old horse left behind to be fed and watered, while the man and his fresh mount started out.

Each man rode five relays, a total of fifty miles. When one man had traveled his fifty miles another rider continued the journey. Under this system it took about eight days for mail from Missouri to reach California, and it cost several dollars to send one letter.

Telegraph lines and the railroads soon supplied much better and faster means of communication. Today a letter can travel from New York to California in one day by air and in three or four days by railroad.

In its time, however, the Pony Express served a useful purpose.

Quarter Horse

The cowboys are rounding up the herd. Things go along smoothly until suddenly one steer decides to trot off on his own. What the cowboys need are horses who can turn about at the drop of a hat, race off after the wandering steer and guide him back to position. A Quarter Horse is perfect for the job. Fast, intelligent, obedient and easily trained, the Quarter Horse is the cowboys' favorite.

Many years ago, in the early days of the South, the Quarter Horse got his name. Plantation owners amused themselves in those days by holding short races. They found that their horses, descended from an English breed, could run a quarter of a mile faster than almost any other type of horse. After this short sprint the horse would tire. So they named this breed the Quarter Horse.

Shetland Pony

All boys and girls love the Shetland Pony with his fine disposition. He makes such a good companion and it is such fun to ride him. Country boys and girls often have ponies of their own — but city children usually ride the ponies at the zoo or at a carnival passing through the town.

The Shetland Pony stands waiting — small, sturdy, patient and good-natured — for some boy or girl to mount him. Sometimes he is hitched to a little cart which holds four or five children.

There are two types of Shetland Ponies: the English, a sturdy, stocky animal, and the American, which is a lighter and more slender pony. The Shetland Pony remains small, no matter what his age, which makes him perfect for children.

Steeplechaser

Steeplechasing originated in England as a race across country from a given point to the nearest church steeple. Today it is a fast and dangerous race over high hedges and wide water jumps. Both the horse and his rider need courage and daring to tackle the thrilling jumps, for one misstep will send them down in a heap.

The course over which the Steeplechase is run is rugged. In the first two miles there are twelve fences and in each following mile there are six fences. There is a ditch six feet wide and two feet deep with a four foot fence in each mile of the course, and the rider must also clear a water ditch that is twelve feet wide and two feet deep with a three foot fence guarding it.

With such a tough course to cover it is understandable why in some Steeplechase races, where thirty or forty horses started, as few as one or two of the riders have actually finished the race.

The Steeplechase horse starts his training at the age of four. Until then his muscles are too weak to attempt the strenuous leaps. This is a sport for powerful horses and tough riders. To the spectator it presents a breath-taking sight. The New York Handicap and the Maryland Cup are two of the great Steeplechase races in this country.

Thoroughbred

"I'll race you to the first post." That is not exactly what the race horse says. In fact he says nothing, he just runs for all he's worth trying to beat the other horses to the finish line. Most race horses are of a breed called the Thoroughbred. This type was bred in England for racing and jumping; its speed and daring are valuable in hunting as well.

The Thoroughbred is a beautiful horse. His long, thin neck, his delicate bones, his small and dainty hoofs delight the eye. Unlike tougher, more independent breeds, the Thoroughbred needs constant care and affection. He is seldom mean or stubborn, but a violent noise or rough handling may startle him into running off.

FUNK & WAGNALLS
DICTIONARY
For Young People

commodore to **damage**

KEYS TO PRONUNCIATION

As in the NEW STANDARD DICTIONARY, two pronunciation keys are here used. The first (Key 1) is the Revised Scientific Alphabet; the second (Key 2), made by means of diacritic marks, is such as has long been in use in text-books and in the older dictionaries.

The following table gives the values of the symbols in the two Keys, except those which, because they have their usual English spelling or alphabetic values, are already familiar.

KEY 1	KEY 2	ILLUSTRATIVE WORDS	KEY 1	KEY 2	ILLUSTRATIVE WORDS
ɑ	ä	as in artistic, cartoon.	g	ḡ	as in go, dog, egg, ghost, guard.
ā	ä	as in art, cart, alms, father.	ŋ	ṇ, ng	as in sing, long, ringing, link.
a	ă	as in add, fat, man, lap, baffle.	th	th	as in thin, bath, faith, ether, Luther.
ā	â, ê	as in air, fare, pear, heir, there.	th	th	as in this, with, breathe, rather, either.
ɑ	à	as in ask, chant, dance, fast.	s	s, ç	as in so, house, this, missing, cent, scene, psychology.
e	ĕ	as in get, bell, says, leopard, said, dead, bury, added.	z	z, ş	as in zest, lazy, buzz, was, houses.
ē	ā, ẹ	as in prey, wait, fame, great, neighbor.	ch	ch	as in chin, rich, church, watch.
i	ĭ, ў	as in hit, tin, miss, cyst, physic.	j	j, ġ	as in jet, gin, gist, judge, pigeon.
ī	ē, ĭ, ў	as in police, mete, greet, sea.	sh	sh, çh	as in ship, dish, issue, nation, ocean, function, machine.
o	o	as in obey, window, photo.	ʒ	zh	as in azure, seizure, leisure, vision.
ō	ō	as in go, note, glory, blow, soul, goat, door, beau.	ə	a,e,o,u,y	as in about, final, sofa, over, separate, mystery, guttural, martyrdom (always unstressed).
o	ŏ, ạ	as in not, odd, what, was.			
ọ	ô, ạ	as in or, north, all, haul, walk.			
u	u, o, ŏŏ	as in full, push, could, stood.	ı	a,e,i,u,y	as in habit, senate, surfeit, biscuit, min'ute, menace, average, privilege, valley, Sunday, cities, renew (always unstressed).
ū	u, o, ōō	as in rule, true, food, who, lose.			
u	ŭ, ŏ	as in but, under, son, other.			
ū	û, ē, ĭ, ў	as in burn, cur, earn, whirl, myrrh.			
ai	ī, ў	as in aisle, pine, sign, light, type, height.	H	H	as in loch (Scotch), ach, mich (German).
au	ou, ow	as in sauerkraut, out, now.			
iu	ū	as in duration, futility.	ü	ü	as in Lübeck (German), Dumas (French).
iū	ū	as in feud, pupil, beauty.			
ei	ŏi, ŏy	as in oil, coin, boy, oyster, loyal.	ṅ	ṅ	as in bon (French).
k	k, c	as in kin, cat, back, ache, pique, quit.			

Of the consonantal and semivowel symbols b, d, f, h, l, m, n, p, r, t, v, w, y, and z, these as initials have the familiar and unmistakable sounds heard in be, do, fee, he, let, met, net, pet, red, ten, vow, wet, yet, and zest; as finals, l, m, n, and r have the sounds heard in able, prism, fasten, flour.

The foreign sounds (H, ü, ṅ) can not be represented in English spellings, but must be described in detail.

H is made with the tongue almost in position for k (as in look). The difference is that for H the tongue does not wholly close the passage, so that the breath rushes out with great friction, making a sound like a very rough h. If the vowel preceding H is made in the front of the mouth (as German i, e, ü, ä), the H is also forward, and is then made by forcing the breath out while the tongue is held firmly in the initial position for English y.

ü represents a sound made by pronouncing ī (the vowel-sound of see), with the lips at the same time fully pursed or rounded as for whistling. It may be noted, also, that the foreign sound represented in this dictionary by the symbol ū (as French danseuse, daṅ″sūz′) is not exactly the vowel heard in the English burn, earn, etc., but is approximately that vowel sounded while the lips are fully pursed or rounded.

ṅ is a symbol indicating that the n itself is silent, but has imparted a nasal quality to the preceding vowel.

The **Abbreviations** used throughout the text of this book will be found explained in their respective places in the dictionary vocabulary.

‡ After a bold-face word, as **Annam, Anam** ‡, indicates that the word to which it is attached is sometimes used.

com'mo-dore, 1 kŏm'o-dōr; 2 ĕŏm'o-dôr, *n.* **1.** In the U. S. Navy, an officer between captain and rear-admiral who is no longer in active service. **2.** In the British Navy, the commander of a squadron. **3.** A title given by courtesy to the senior captain of a naval squadron, or merchant fleet, or to a yacht-club president.

com'mon, 1 kŏm'ən; 2 ĕŏm'on. **I.** *a.* [*com'mon-er; com'mon-est.*] **1.** Often happening or seen; usual. **2.** Belonging to everybody or to all of a group; as, *common* property; *common* knowledge. **3.** Vulgar. **4.** Not having rank or position; as, the *common* people. **II.** *n.* **1.** Land owned by a town or open to the use of all. **2.** The average or usual. —**in common**, belonging to all; alike; as, we three have much *in common.* — **com'mon-ly**, *adv.* — **com'mon-ness**, *n.*
SYN.: coarse, customary, frequent, mutual.

com'mon-er, 1 kŏm'ən-ər; 2 ĕŏm'on-er, *n.* One of the common people.

com'mon noun. A noun that applies to any of a class; as, "girl" is a *common noun*.

com'mon-place", 1 kŏm'ən-plēs"; 2 ĕŏm'on-plāç". **I.** *a.* Not interesting; ordinary. **II.** *n.* Something that is ordinary and familiar, not new or interesting. —**com'mon-place "ness**, *n.*

com'mon-weal", 1 kŏm'ən-wīl"; 2 ĕŏm'on-wēl", *n.* The general welfare.

com'mon-wealth", 1 kŏm'ən-welfh"; 2 ĕŏm'on-wĕlth", *n.* **1.** The people of a state; the state itself. **2.** A republic; a state in which the people rule.

com-mo'tion, 1 kə-mō'shən; 2 ĕŏ-mō'shon, *n.* Great confusion; excitement; disturbance; as, his arrival caused a *commotion*.

com'mu-nal, 1 kŏm'yu-nəl *or* kə-miū'nəl; 2 ĕŏm'yu-nal *or* ĕŏ-mū'nal, *a.* Belonging to all of a community; public.

com-mune', 1 kə-miūn'; 2 ĕŏ-mūn', *vi.* [*com-muned'; com-mun'ing.*] **1.** To talk or feel intimately with; to have fellowship with. **2.** To take communion.

com'mune, 1 kŏm'yūn; 2 ĕŏm'yun, *n.* **1.** The smallest political division of France, governed by a mayor and a council. **2.** A self-governing community.

com-mu'ni-ca-ble, 1 kə-miū'nı-kə-bl; 2 ĕŏ-mū'ni-ea-bl, *a.* Able to be told or taken from one person to another; as, a *communicable* idea; a *communicable* disease. —**com-mu "ni-ca-bil'i-ty**, *n.*

com-mu'ni-cant, 1 kə-miū'nı-kənt; 2 ĕŏ-mū'ni-eant, *n.* One who takes communion (the Lord's Supper); one who belongs to the church.

com-mu'ni-cate, 1 kə-miū'nı-kēt; 2 ĕŏ-mū'ni-eāt, *v.* [*com-mu'ni-cat"ed; com-mu'ni-cat"ing.*] **I.** *t.* To transfer or give to another; to make known; as, to *communicate* one's plans to a friend. **II.** *i.* **1.** To have contact with or be in touch with; as, to *communicate* with some one by telephone. **2.** To take communion (the Lord's Supper.) —**com-mu'ni-ca"tor**, *n.*

com-mu"ni-ca'tion, 1 kə-miū"nı-kē'shən; 2 ĕŏ-mū"ni-eā'shon, *n.* **1.** The act of communicating; as, *communication* of a disease. **2.** Contact by conferences, letters, messages, etc.; as, to keep in *communication*. **3.** A letter or message. **4.** A means of communicating, such as a highway, a passage, mails, telegraph. —**com-mu'ni-ca-tive**, *a.* —**com-mu'ni-ca-tive-ly**, *adv.* —**com-mu'ni-ca-tive-ness**, *n.*

com-mu'nion, 1 kə-miūn'yən; 2 ĕŏ-mūn'yon, *n.* **1.** Fellowship; as, *communion* with nature or with a close friend. **2.** The sacrament or the partaking of it. See *sacrament*. **3.** A denomination of Christians; as, the Methodist, or Baptist *communion*.

com'mu-nism, 1 kŏm'yu-nizm; 2 ĕŏm'yu-nĭşm, *n.* **1.** A social system in which there is community of goods. **2.** A theory of government under which property and production are held as a common trust and the profits arising from all labor devoted to the general good. **3.** A doctrine or practise calling for the abolition of all private property ownership, and the absolute control by the community in all matters relating to labor, religion, social relations, etc. —**com'mu-nist**, *n.* An advocate of communism. —**com "mu-nis'tic**, *a.* — **com "mu-nis'tic-al-ly**, *adv.*

com-mu'ni-ty, 1 kə-miū'nı-tı; 2 ĕŏ-mū'ni-ty, *n.* [*com-mu'ni-ties*, pl.] **1.** A group of people having the same interests or living in the same neighborhood, village, town, or state. **2.** A sharing; likeness; as, a *community* of interests.

com"mu-ta'tion, 1 kŏm"yū-tē'shən; 2 ĕŏm"yu-tā'shon, *n.* **1.** A substitution of one kind of payment or service for another. **2.** Reduction of a prisoner's punishment. —**com "mu-ta'tion tic'ket**. A railway or other ticket good for a certain number of trips within a certain length of time at a cheaper rate than the ordinary ticket.

com'mu-ta"tor, 1 kŏm'yū-tē"tər; 2 ĕŏm'yu-tā"tor, *n.* A device to change an electric current in direction or strength.

com-mute', 1 kə-miūt'; 2 ĕŏ-mūt', *v.* [*com-mut'ed; com-mut'ing.*] **I.** *t.* To exchange; to substitute something less; as, to *commute* a murderer's sentence. **II.** *i.* To travel on a commutation ticket. —**com-mut'er**, *n.*

com-pact', 1 kəm-pakt'; 2 ĕŏm-pǎet', *vt.* **1.** To pack closely. **2.** To compose.

com-pact', *a.* **1.** Closely united; solid;

dense; as, a *compact* crowd. **2.** Condensed; brief; putting much in a small space. — **com-pact′ly,** *adv.* —**com-pact′ness,** *n.*

com′pact[1], 1 kəm′pakt; 2 cŏm′păet, *n.* An agreement.

com′pact[2] *n.* A small case fitted with a mirror and in which women carry face= powder and sometimes rouge.

com-pan′ion, 1 kəm-pan′yən; 2 cŏm-păn′yon, *n.* A person or thing that accompanies; a comrade. —**com-pan′ion,** *vt.* & *vi.* SYN.: ally, friend, partner.

com-pan′ion-a-ble, 1 kəm-pan′yən-ə-bl; 2 cŏm-păn′yon-a-bl, *a.* Sociable; agreeable. —**com-pan′ion-a-bly,** *adv.*

com-pan′ion-ship, 1 kəm-pan′yən-ship; 2 cŏm-păn′yon-shĭp, *n.* Fellowship; association; company.

com-pan′ion-way″, *n.* A staircase leading down from the deck of a ship.

com′pa-ny, 1 kum′pə-nı; 2 cŏm′pa-ny, *n.* [*com′pa-nies,* pl.] **1.** The society or presence of another or others. **2.** One or more guests. **3.** A business partnership or a group of people working together; as, a *company* of actors. **4.** A body of soldiers commanded by a captain. —**com′pa-ny,** *a.*

com′pa-ra-ble, 1 kəm′pə-rə-bl; 2 cŏm′-pa-ra-bl, *a.* Fit to be compared; similar. —**com′pa-ra-bly,** *adv.*

com-par′a-tive, 1 kəm-par′ə-tıv; 2 cŏm-păr′a-tiv. **I.** *a.* **1.** Of, using, or resulting from comparison. **2.** Relative; as, an act of *comparative* importance. **3.** Expressing a higher or lower degree of the quality denoted by an adjective or adverb; as, ''slower'' is the *comparative* degree of ''slow.'' **II.** *n.* The comparative degree of an adjective or adverb. See *degree,* 3. —**com-par′a-tive-ly,** *adv.*

com-pare′, 1 kəm-pār′; 2 cŏm-pâr′, *v.* [*com-pared′; com-par′ing.*] **I.** *t.* **1.** To examine persons or things in order to see or to show their likenesses or differences. **2.** To liken; as, to *compare* a brave man to a lion. **3.** To give the degrees of comparison for an adjective or adverb. **II.** *i.* To be worthy of comparison.

com-pare′, *n.* Comparison; as, *beyond compare.*

com-par′i-son, 1 kəm-par′ı-sən; 2 cŏm-păr′i-son, *n.* **1.** An estimate of relative likeness or difference; an example. **2.** The forms of an adjective or adverb which show degrees of more or less.

com-part′ment, 1 kəm-pārt′ment *or* -mənt; 2 cŏm-pärt′ment, *n.* A separate section or division of a thing.

com′pass, 1 kum′pəs; 2 cŏm′pas. **I.** *vt.* **1.** To get possession of; to attain; as, to *compass* one's ambitions. **2.** To comprehend; as, the mind can not *compass* large numbers easily. **3.** To surround. **II.** *n.* **1.** An instrument with a magnetic needle which always points north. **2.** An instrument for drawing circles, usually called **compasses. 3.** Extent; space; range. **4.** Boundary.

Types of Compass.
Mariners' compass (1). Bow=spring pen=compass (2).

com-pas′sion, 1 kəm-pash′ən; 2 cŏm-păsh′on, *n.* Pity for suffering with desire to help or to spare. —**com-pas′sion-ate,** *a.* — **com-pas′sion-ate-ly,** *adv.*

com-pat′i-ble, 1 kəm-pat′ı-bl; 2 cŏm-păt′i-bl, *a.* Capable of existing together; harmonious; congenial. —**com-pat″i-bil′i-ty,** *n.* —**com-pat′i-bly,** *adv.*

com-pa′tri-ot, 1 kəm-pē′trı-ət; 2 cŏm-pā′tri-ot, *n.* A fellow countryman.

com-peer′, 1 kəm-pır′; 2 cŏm-pēr′, *n.* One of equal rank; a comrade; an associate.

com-pel′, 1 kəm-pel′; 2 cŏm-pĕl′, *vt.* [*com-pelled′; com-pel′ling.*] **1.** To drive or force. **2.** To obtain by force; as, the law *compels* obedience. —**com-pel′ling-ly,** *adv.* SYN.: coerce, drive, necessitate, oblige.

com′pen-sate, 1 kəm′pen-sēt; 2 cŏm′-pĕn-sāt, *v.* [*com′pen-sat″ed; com′pen-sat″-ing.*] **I.** *t.* **1.** To make suitable pay or reward to; as, to *compensate* a man for his work. **2.** To make amends to; as, the railroad *compensated* its passengers for injuries received in a wreck. **II.** *i.* To make amends for; to balance. —**com″-pen-sa′tion,** *n.* —**com-pen′sa-tive, com-pen′sa-to-ry,** *a.* Serving as compensation.

com-pete′, 1 kəm-pīt′; 2 cŏm-pēt′, *vi.* [*com-pet′ed; com-pet′ing.*] To try to win against another person or other persons; as, to *compete* for a prize.

com′pe-tence, 1 kəm′pı-tens; 2 cŏm′pe-tĕnç, *n.* **1.** Ability; as, *competence* in work. **2.** Enough to live on; as, her father left her a *competence* when he died. **com′pe-ten-cy** ‡.

com′pe-tent, 1 kəm′pı-tent; 2 cŏm′pe-tĕnt, *a.* Capable; able; qualified; as, a *competent* teacher. —**com′pe-tent-ly,** *adv.*

com″pe-ti′tion, 1 kəm″pı-tish′ən; 2 cŏm″pe-tĭsh′on, *n.* **1.** The rivalry or struggle of two or more persons for the same thing or for superiority. **2.** Trial of skill, as in sport; test of ability, as in games. SYN.: contest, emulation, opposition, strife.

com-pet′i-tive, 1 kəm-pet′ı-tıv; 2 cŏm-pĕt′i-tiv, *a.* Characterized by competition; as, a *competitive* examination. —**com-pet′i-tive-ly,** *adv.* —**com-pet′i-tive-ness,** *n.*

com-pet′i-tor, 1 kəm-pet′ı-tər; 2 cŏm-pĕt′i-tor, *n.* One that competes.

com-pile′, 1 kəm-pail′; 2 cŏm-pīl′, *vt.* [*com-piled′; com-pil′ing.*] **1.** To compose (usually a book) from other writings; as, to *compile* a history of a town from its old records. **2.** To collect writings into a new form. —**com″pi-la′tion,** *n.* —**com-pil′er,** *n.*

com-pla′cence, 1 kəm-plē′sens; 2 cŏm-plā′çĕnç, *n.* Satisfaction; self=approval. **com-pla′cen-cy** ‡. — **com-pla′cent,** *a.* —**com-pla′cent-ly,** *adv.*

com-plain′, 1 kəm-plēn′; 2 cŏm-plān′, *vi.* **1.** To express pain, grief, or a feeling that one has been badly treated; to find fault. **2.** To enter a legal complaint. — **com-plain′er,** *n.* —**com-plain′ing,** *a.* — **com-plain′ing-ly,** *adv.*

SYN.: growl, grumble, lament, remonstrate.

com-plain′ant, 1 kəm-plēn′ənt; 2 cŏm-plān′ant, *n.* One who brings charges in court.

com-plaint′, *n.* **1.** A statement of wrong or injury. **2.** Expressions of pain, grief, or mistreatment. **3.** A reason to complain. **4.** A physical ailment; disease.

com′plai-sance″, 1 kəm′plē-zɑns″ *or* kəm-plē′zəns; 2 cŏm′plā-sänç″ *or* cŏm-plā′şanç, *n.* The desire to please; politeness.

com′plai-sant″, 1 kəm′plē-zant″ *or* kəm-plē′zənt; 2 cŏm′plā-şänt″ *or* cŏm-plā′şant, *a.* Showing a desire to please. — **com′plai-sant″ly,** *a.* —**com′plai-sant″-ness,** *n.*

com′ple-ment, 1 kəm′plı-ment *or* -mənt; 2 cŏm′ple-ment. **I.** *vt.* To make complete. **II.** *n.* **1.** Full number; as, the vessel has her *complement* of men. **2.** That which completes; the state of completion.

com″ple-men′ta-ry, 1 kəm″plı-men′tə-rı; 2 cŏm″ple-mĕn′ta-ry, *a.* Completing; providing each other's needs. **com″ple-men′tal** ‡. —**complementary angles,** two angles which together form a right angle.

com-plete′, 1 kəm-plīt′; 2 cŏm-plēt′. **I.** *vt.* [*com-plet′ed; com-plet′ing.*] To finish; to fulfil; to accomplish. **II.** *a.* Finished; perfect; full; whole. — **com-plete′ly,** *adv.* —**com-plete′ness,** *n.*

SYN.: close, conclude, effect, end, terminate.

com-ple′tion, 1 kəm-plī′shən; 2 cŏm-plē′shon, *n.* The act of completing or the state of being complete. —**com-ple′tive,** *a.*

com′plex, 1 kəm′pleks *or* kəm-pleks′; 2 cŏm′plĕks *or* cŏm-plĕks′, *a.* **1.** Consisting of various parts; as, a *complex* sentence. **2.** Complicated; involved; hard to understand. —**com-plex′ly,** *adv.*

SYN.: complicated, difficult, intricate.

com-plex′ion, 1 kəm-plek′shən; 2 cŏm-plĕk′shon, *n.* **1.** The color and appearance of the skin, especially of the face. **2.** General appearance; quality; as, the *complexion* of events. —**com-plex′ioned,** *a.*

com-plex′i-ty, 1 kəm-pleks′ı-tı; 2 cŏm-plĕks′i-ty, *n.* [*com-plex′i-ties,* pl.] The state of being complex.

com-pli′ance, 1 kəm-plai′əns; 2 cŏm-plī′anç, *n.* Willingness to yield to the wishes or commands of another. **com-pli′an-cy** ‡. —**com-pli′ant,** *a.* —**com-pli′ant-ly,** *adv.*

com′pli-cate, 1 kəm′plı-kēt; 2 cŏm′pli-eāt, *vt.* [*com′pli-cat″ed; com′pli-cat″ing.*] To make difficult or puzzling; to mix; to confuse. —**com′pli-cat″ed,** *a.* —**com″pli-ca′tion,** *n.*

com-plic′i-ty, 1 kəm-plis′ı-tı; 2 cŏm-plĭç′i-ty, *n.* [*com-plic′i-ties,* pl.] Assistance in doing something wrong; a share in a crime; as, *complicity* in murder.

com′pli-ment, 1 kəm′plı-ment *or* -mənt; 2 cŏm′pli-ment. **I.** *vt.* To express admiration or congratulation; as, to *compliment* a man on his success. **II.** *n.* **1.** An expression of praise, admiration, congratulation, etc. **2.** A greeting or remembrance (usually plural); as, give him my *compliments.*

com″pli-men′ta-ry, 1 kəm″plı-men′tə-rı; 2 cŏm″pli-mĕn′ta-ry, *a.* **1.** Approving or praising; as, a *complimentary* remark. **2.** Given as a courtesy; as, *complimentary* tickets were given to parents.

com-ply′, 1 kəm-plai′; 2 cŏm-plȳ′, *vi.* [*com-plied′; com-ply′ing.*] To follow a command or a request.

SYN.: agree, assent, obey, submit.

com-po′nent, 1 kəm-pō′nent; 2 cŏm-pō′nĕnt. **I.** *a.* Forming a part of; composing; as, the *component* parts of a sentence are subject, verb, etc. **II.** *n.* A part; as, the *components* of a mixture.

com-port′, 1 kəm-pērt′; 2 cŏm-pôrt′, *v.* **I.** *t.* To behave; as, to *comport* oneself properly. **II.** *i.* To agree; to suit.

com-pose′ 1 kəm-pōz′; 2 cŏm-pōş′, *vt.* [*com-posed′; com-pos′ing.*] **1.** To construct; especially, to make up of different parts; as, to *compose* music. **2.** To form by being united with. **3.** To calm; as, to *compose* oneself in time of danger. **4.** To reconcile; arrange; settle; as, to *compose* differences. —**com-posed′,** *a.* Calm. —**com-pos′ed-ly,** *adv.* —**com-pos′ed-ness,** *n.*

com-pos′er, 1 kəm-pōz′ər; 2 cŏm-pōş′er, *n.* One who composes, especially music.

com-pos′ite, 1 kəm-pez′ıt; 2 cŏm-pŏş′it. **I.** *a.* Made up of different parts; mixed. **II.** *n.* Something having different parts; a combination. —**com-pos′ite-ly,** *adv.*

com″po-si′tion, 1 kəm″po-zish′ən; 2 cŏm″po-şish′on, *n.* **1.** The act of composing; as, the *composition* of an opera. **2.**

A literary, artistic, or musical production. **3.** Make-up; contents. **4.** Typesetting.

com-pos′i-tor, 1 kəm-pɒz′ı-tər; 2 cŏm-pŏg′ı-tor, *n.* A typesetter.

com′post, 1 kəm′pōst; 2 cŏm′pōst, *n.* A mixture, as for fertilizing or for plastering.

com-po′sure, 1 kəm-pō′ʒur; 2 cŏm-pō′zhụr, *n.* Calmness.

com′pote, 1 kəm′pōt; 2 cŏm′pōt, *n.* Stewed or preserved fruit.

com-pound′, 1 kəm-paund′; 2 cŏm-pound′, *vt.* To make by mixing; as, to *compound* a medicine.

SYN.: blend, combine, merge, mingle, unite.

com′pound, 1 kəm′paund; 2 cŏm′-pound, *a.* Having two or more parts. A **compound sentence** contains two or more independent clauses in combination, as in "snow fell and the wind blew."

SYN.: combined, composite, mixed.

com′pound¹, *n.* Something having two or more parts; a mixture.

com′pound², *n.* In the Orient, property with buildings enclosed by a wall.

com″pre-hend′, 1 kəm″prı-hend′; 2 cŏm″pre-hĕnd′, *vt.* **1.** To grasp mentally; to understand fully. **2.** To include; as, the word "airship" *comprehends* both airplanes and dirigibles.

SYN.: comprise, embody, know, perceive.

com″pre-hen′si-ble, 1 kəm″prı-hen′-sı-bl; 2 cŏm″pre-hĕn′si-bl, *a.* Able to be understood. —**com″pre-hen″si-bil′i-ty,** *n.* —**com″pre-hen′si-bly,** *adv.*

com″pre-hen′sion, 1 kəm″prı-hen′-shən; 2 cŏm″pre-hĕn′shon, *n.* Ability to understand; as, a *comprehension* of art.

com″pre-hen′-sive, 1 kəm″prı-hen′-sıv; 2 cŏm″pre-hĕn′siv, *a.* **1.** Including much; as, a *comprehensive* study of literature. **2.** Able to understand. —**com″pre-hen′sive-ly,** *adv.* —**com″pre-hen′sive-ness,** *n.*

com-press′, 1 kəm-pres′; 2 cŏm-prĕs′, *vt.* To press together or into smaller space; to condense. —**com-press″i-bil′i-ty,** *n.* —**com-press′i-ble,** *a.* —**com-pres′sion,** *n.* —**com-pres′sive,** *a.* —**com-pres′sive-ly,** *adv.*

com′press, 1 kəm′pres; 2 cŏm′prĕs, *n.* **1.** A device for compressing. **2.** A soft pad or a wet cloth applied to the body.

com-prise′, ⎰1 kəm-praiz′; 2 cŏm-prīg′, **com-prize′,** ⎱ *vt.* [*com-prised′; com-pris′-ing.*] To include; to consist of; as, a statement *comprising* all the facts on the matter. —**com-pri′sal,** *n.*

com′pro-mise, 1 kəm′pro-maiz; 2 cŏm′-pro-mig, *v.* [*com′pro-mised; com′pro-mis″-ing.*] **I.** *t.* **1.** To settle by giving up something on both sides; as, to *compromise* a dispute. **2.** To expose to suspicion; as, his presence at the time of the robbery *com-promised* him. **II.** *i.* To make a settlement

by which both sides give up something.

com′pro-mise, *n.* A settlement by which both sides give up something.

comp-trol′ler, 1 kən-trōl′ər; 2 cŏn-trōl′er, *n.* Same as *controller.*

com-pul′sion, 1 kəm-pul′shən; 2 ŏm-pul′shon, *n.* The use of force; the state of being compelled or forced.

com-pul′so-ry, 1 kəm-pul′so-rı; 2 cŏm-pul′so-ry, *a.* **1.** Compelling; as, a *compulsory* command. **2.** Required; enforced; as, going to school is *compulsory* in the United States. —**com-pul′so-ri-ly,** *adv.*

com-punc′tion, 1 kəm-puŋk′shən; 2 cŏm-puŋe′shon, *n.* Self-reproach for wrongdoing; slight regret. —**com-punc′tious,** *a.*

com-pute′, 1 kəm-piūt′; 2 cŏm-pūt′, *vt.* [*com-put′ed; com-put′ing.*] To figure by using numbers; to calculate. —**com-put′a-ble,** *a.* —**com″pu-ta′tion,** *n.* —**com-put′-er,** *n.*

com′rade, 1 kəm′rad; 2 cŏm′răd, *n.* A close friend or a companion in work. —**com′rade-ship,** *n.* **com′rade-ry†.**

con, 1 kən; 2 cŏn, *vt.* [*conned; con′ning.*] To study with care; to read; to learn.

con. I. *n.* Argument against (often plural); as, to argue the pros and *cons* of a question. **II.** *adv.* Against; as, to discuss a matter pro and *con.*

con-, *prefix.* With; together; a form of *com-* before *c, d, f, g, i, j, n, q, s, t, w;* as, *con*dense, *con*fer, *con*join.

con′cave, 1 kən′kēv; 2 cŏn′eāv, *a.* Hollow and rounded like the inside of a ball or a bowl or a spoon. —**con′cave-ly,** *adv.*

con-cav′i-ty, 1 kən-kav′ı-tı; 2 cŏn-eāv′i-ty, *n.* [*con-cav′i-ties,* pl.] **1.** The state of being concave. **2.** A hollow.

con-ceal′, 1 kən-sīl′; 2 cŏn-çēl′, *vt.* To hide. —**con-ceal′a-ble,** *a.* —**con-ceal′-ment,** *n.*

SYN.: cover, screen, secrete, shelter.

con-cede′, 1 kən-sīd′; 2 cŏn-çēd′, *vt.* [*con-ced′ed; con-ced′ing.*] **1.** To admit; to acknowledge; as, to *concede* a point in an argument. **2.** To bestow; to grant; as, to *concede* a man the right to fish.

SYN.: abandon, allow, yield.

con-ceit, 1 kən-sīt′; 2 cŏn-çēt′, *n.* **1.** Too high an opinion of oneself; vanity. **2.** A fanciful idea; a clever thought or expression. **3.** Understanding; conception; opinion. —**con-ceit′ed,** *a.* **-ly,** *adv.* **-ness,** *n.*

con-ceive′, 1 kən-sīv′; 2 cŏn-çēv′, *v.* [*con-ceived′; con-ceiv′ing.*] **I.** *t.* **1.** To form an idea of; as, to *conceive* the importance of a decision. **2.** To become possessed with; as, to *conceive* a dislike. **3.** To think of; to understand; to imagine; as, to *conceive* a plan. **4.** To become pregnant with. **II.** *i.* **1.** To think; to imagine. **2.** To become pregnant. — **con-ceiv′a-ble**, *a.* — **con-ceiv′a-bly**, *adv.*

con′cen-trate, 1 kən′sen-trēt; 2 cŏn′-çĕn-trāt, *v.* [*con′cen-trat″ed; con′cen-trat″-ing.*] **I.** *t.* **1.** To bring to a center; fix; as, to *concentrate* attention on algebra. **2.** To make smaller in amount but stronger; to condense; as, to *concentrate* a food. **II.** *i.* **1.** To come to a center. **2.** To pay particular attention; to fix the mind on one thing.

con″cen-tra′tion, 1 kən″sen-trē′shən; 2 cŏn″çĕn-trā′shon, *n.* The act of concentrating or that which is concentrated.

con-cen′tric, 1 kən-sen′trık; 2 cŏn-çĕn′-trıc, *a.* Having the same center; as, *concentric* circles. — **con″cen-tric′i-ty**, *n.*

con′cept, 1 kən′sept; 2 cŏn′çĕpt, *n.* A general idea or thought.

con-cep′tion, 1 kən-sep′shən; 2 cŏn-çĕp′shon, *n.* **1.** An idea. **2.** The act of conceiving. — **con-cep′tu-al**, *a.* — **con-cep′tu-al-ly**, *adv.*

con-cern′, 1 kən-sūrn′; 2 cŏn-çĕrn′. **I.** *vt.* & *vi.* **1.** To relate or belong to; to be of interest or importance to; as, your affairs do not *concern* me. **2.** To occupy or engage; as, he *concerned* himself with banking. **3.** To worry; as, his poor health *concerns* me. **II.** *n.* **1.** That which concerns one. **2.** Interest; worry; as, causing *concern.* **3.** A business firm. — **con-cerned′**, *a.* Syn.: affair, anxiety, care, interest.

con-cern′ing, 1 kən-sūrn′ıŋ; 2 cŏn-çĕrn′ing, *prep.* About; in relation to.

con-cert′, 1 kən-sūrt′; 2 cŏn-çĕrt′, *vt.* To arrange in concert. — **con-cert′ed**, *a.*

con′cert, 1 kən′sūrt; 2 cŏn′çĕrt, *n.* **1.** A musical performance. **2.** Harmony; agreement; unity; as, working or speaking in *concert.* — **con′cert**, *a.*

con″cer-ti′na, 1 kən″sər-tī′nə; 2 cŏn″-çer-tī′na, *n.* A small musical instrun.ent of the accordion class.

con-cer′to, 1 kən-cher′[*or* -sūr′]to; 2 cŏn-chĕr′[*or* -çĕr′]to, *n.* A musical composition for one or more instruments accompanied by an orchestra.

con-ces′sion, 1 kən-sesh′ən; 2 cŏn-çĕsh′on, *n.* The act of conceding, or that which is conceded. — **con-ces′-sive**, *a.*

conch, 1 kɒŋk; 2 cǫ̆ne, *n.* A large spiral marine-shell.

con-cil′i-ate, 1 kən-sıl′-ı-ēt; 2 cŏn-çĭl′ı-āt, *vt.* [*con-cil′i-at″ed; con-cil′i-at″ing.*]
To overcome the hostility of; to soothe; to reconcile; as, to *conciliate* an enemy. — **con-cil″i-a′tion**, *n.* — **con-cil″i-a′tor**, *n.* — **con-cil′i-a-to-ry**, *a.*

con-cise′, 1 kən-sais′; 2 cŏn-çīs′, *a.*

Conch.

Expressing much in brief form. — **con-cise′ly**, *adv.* — **con-cise′ness**, *n.*
Syn.: compact, pithy, short, succinct, terse.

con′clave, 1 kən′klēv; 2 cŏn′clāv, *n.* A secret meeting or society.

con-clude′, 1 kən-klūd′; 2 cŏn-clųd′, *v.* [*con-clud′ed; con-clud′ing.*] **I.** *t.* **1.** To arrive at by reasoning; as, I *concluded* from his manner that he was guilty. **2.** To finish. **3.** To settle; as, to *conclude* a treaty. **II.** *i.* To come to an end.
Syn.: complete, deduce, infer, terminate.

con-clu′sion, 1 kən-klū′zən; 2 cŏn-clų′-zhon, *n.* **1.** The end; as, the *conclusion* of a book. **2.** A final decision; as, to reach a *conclusion* that hard work is necessary. **3.** A settlement; as, the *conclusion* of a treaty.

con-clu′sive, 1 kən-klū′sıv; 2 cŏn-clų′-sıv, *a.* Decisive; putting an end to doubt. — **con-clu′sive-ly**, *adv.* — **con-clu′sive-ness**, *n.*

con-coct′, 1 kən-kɒkt′; 2 cŏn-cŏct′, *vt.* To prepare by mixing; to plan; to scheme; as, to *concoct* a candy. — **con-coc′tion**, *n.*

con-com′i-tant, 1 kən-kɒm′ı-tənt; 2 cŏn-cŏm′i-tant. **I.** *a.* Existing or happening together; as, *concomitant* evils. **II.** *n.* A thing which happens with another thing. — **con-com′i-tant-ly**, *adv.*

con′cord, 1 kəŋ′kērd; 2 cŏṇ′côrd, *n.* Agreement; accord; harmony.

Con′cord, *n.* **1.** A village in Massachusetts where the first battle of the American Revolution was fought. **2.** The capital city of New Hampshire.

con-cor′dance, 1 kən-kēr′dəns; 2 cŏn-côr′danç, *n.* **1.** Agreement. **2.** An index of words or topics in a book, as the Bible.

con′course, 1 kən′kērs; 2 cŏn′côrs, *n.* **1.** A moving together; as, a *concourse* of waters. **2.** An assembly; a crowd. **3.** A place, usually open, where a crowd gathers.

con′crete, 1 kən′krīt *or* kən-krīt′; 2 cŏn′-erēt *or* cŏn-erēt′, *a.* **1.** Having actual existence; real: opposed to *abstract*; as, a chair is a *concrete* thing but hope is an abstract idea. **2.** Particular; definite; as, a *concrete* example. **3.** Made of concrete. — **con′crete-ly**, *adv.* — **con′crete-ness**, *n.*

con′crete, *n.* A hard mixture, as of gravel or sand, with cement and water.

con′cu-bine, 1 kəŋ′kiū-bain; 2 cŏṇ′cū-bīn, *n.* One who is not the first or legal wife; a secondary wife, in countries where a man may have more than one.

con-cur′, 1 kən-kūr′; 2 cŏn-eûr′, *vi.* [*con-curred′; con-cur′ring.*] **1.** To come together. **2.** To agree; as, to *concur* in an opinion.

con-cur′rence, 1 kən-kūr′ens; 2 cŏn-eûr′ĕnç, *n.* **1.** Combination or coming together. **2.** Agreement. **3.** Coincidence; a happening at the same time. — **con-cur′rent**, *a.* — **con-cur′rent-ly**, *adv.*

con-cus'sion, 1 kən-kuѕh'ən; 2 cŏn-cuѕh'on, *n.* A violent shaking; a shock; a jar; especially, a shock to some part of the body by a fall or blow; as, *concussion* of the brain. **—con-cus'sive,** *a.*

con-demn', 1 kən-dem'; 2 cŏn-dĕm', *vt.* [*con-demned'; con-demn'ing.*] **1.** To speak against; to prove to be wrong; to disapprove; as, people *condemn* dishonesty. **2.** To pronounce sentence against; as, to *condemn* a murderer to death. **3.** To forbid officially the use of something as unfit; as, to *condemn* a building because of danger from fire. **4.** To take over for public use; as, to *condemn* land. **—con"dem-na'tion,** *n.*
Syn.: censure, denounce, doom, sentence.

con"den-sa'tion, 1 kən"den-sē'shən; 2 cŏn"dĕn-sā'shon, *n.* The act or product of condensing.

con-dense', 1 ken-dens'; 2 cŏn-dĕns', *v.* [*con-densed'; con-dens'ing.*] I. *t.* **1.** To reduce the bulk of; make dense; compress; as, to *condense* a long speech into a few paragraphs; to *condense* milk. **2.** To change from a gas or vapor to a solid or liquid. II. *i.* To become condensed.

con-dens'er, 1 kən-dens'ər; 2 cŏn-dĕns'er, *n.* **1.** One who or that which condenses. **2.** A device for condensing or collecting anything, as steam or electricity.

con"de-scend', 1 kən"dı-send'; 2 cŏn"de-sĕnd', *vi.* **1.** To be gracious or kind to one of lower rank; as, the king *condescended* to speak to the woodcutter. **2.** To do something unworthy of oneself. **— con"de-scend'ing,** *a.* **—con"de-scend'ing-ly,** *adv.*

con"de-scen'sion, 1 kən"dı-sen'shən; 2 cŏn"de-sĕn'shon, *n.* The act of condescending; courtesy to inferiors.

con'di-ment, 1 kən'dı-mĕnt *or* -mənt; 2 cŏn'di-ment, *n.* A sauce, relish, spice, etc., used to flavor food.

con-di'tion, 1 kən-dish'ən; 2 cŏn-dĭsh'on. I. *vt.* **1.** To place a condition on; as, he *conditioned* his departure upon completion of the work. **2.** To be the condition of; as, his consent *conditioned* my going. **3.** To put into satisfactory condition; as, to *condition* an automobile. II. *n.* **1.** The state a person or thing is in; as, a book in good *condition.* **2.** *pl.* Environment; as, poor working *conditions.* **3.** State of health. **4.** A requirement which must be met before something is done; as, my mother's approval was a *condition* of my going. **5.** A grade of rank; social position; as, a man of low *condition.* **—con-di'tion-al,** *a.* **—con-di'tion-al-ly,** *adv.*

con-dole', 1 kən-dōl'; 2 cŏn-dōl', *vi.* [*con-doled'; con-dol'ing.*] To grieve or express sympathy with another. **—con-dol'er,** *n.*

con-do'lence, 1 kən-dō'lens; 2 cŏn-dō'-lĕnç, *n.* Expression of sympathy.

con"do-na'tion, 1 kən"do-nē'shən; 2 cŏn"do-nā'shon, *n.* Forgiveness.

con-done', 1 kən-dōn'; 2 cŏn-dōn', *vt.* [*con-doned'; con-don'ing.*] To treat as overlooked or forgiven; as, to *condone* an error.

con'dor, 1 kən'dər *or* -dôr; 2 cŏn'dor *or* -dôr, *n.* **1.** A large vulture of the high Andes Mountains. **2.** The similar vulture of California.

Condor.

con-duce', 1 kən-diūs'; 2 cŏn-dūç', *vi.* [*con-duced'; con-duc'ing.*] To help or tend toward a result; to contribute; as, fresh air *conduces* to good health. **—con-du'cive,** *a.* **—con-du'cive-ly,** *adv.* **—con-du'cive-ness,** *n.*

con-duct', 1 kən-dukt'; 2 cŏn-dŭct'. I. *vt.* **1.** To go with or show the way; guide; escort. **2.** To manage; carry on; control, as a business. **3.** To direct; behave; as, he *conducted* himself with ease. **4.** To send through or across, as electricity. II. *vi.* **1.** To serve as a conductor. **2.** To direct or lead. **3.** To behave; act. **—con-duct'i-ble,** *a.* Capable of being conducted.

con'duct, 1 kən'dukt; 2 cŏn'dŭct, *n.* **1.** Behavior. **2.** Management; direction.

con-duc'tion, 1 kən-duk'shən; 2 cŏn-dŭç'shon, *n.* The act of sending or carrying through or across, as heat, sound, water, or electricity.

con-duc'tive, 1 kən-duk'tıv; 2 cŏn-dŭç'-tiv, *a.* **1.** Having the power to conduct. **2.** Proceeding by or resulting from conduction. **—con"duc-tiv'i-ty,** *n.*

con-duc'tor, 1 kən-duk'tər; 2 cŏn-dŭç'-tor, *n.* **1.** One who guides or leads; a manager; as, the *conductor* of a tour. **2.** An official in charge of passengers on a railway train, street=car, omnibus, etc., who collects fares or tickets and aids the passengers. **3.** A body having conducting power, as a lightning=rod.

con'duit, 1 kən'dıt *or* -dwit; 2 cŏn'dit *or* -dwĭt, *n.* A means for conducting something; as (1) a tube or pipe for a fluid; (2) an underground passage for wires.

cone, 1 kōn; 2 cŏn, *n.* **1.** A solid figure that tapers uniformly from a circular base to a point; also, any object having such a shape; as, an ice=cream *cone.* **2.** In botany, a dry scaly fruit, as of the pine, containing the seeds.

Cone (2).
1. Stone=pine cone.
2. Swiss pine cone.

co'ney, *n.* [*co'neys,* pl.] Same as *cony.*

con-fec'tion, 1 kən-fek'shən; 2 cŏn-fĕç'-

shon, *n*. A sweet preserve or candy made of fruits and sugar, etc.; a sweetmeat. — **con-fec'tion-er,** *n*. One who makes or deals in confectionery. — **con-fec'tion-er-y** *n*. [*con-fec'tion-er-ies,* pl.] **1.** Candies, sweetmeats, etc., collectively. **2.** A confectioner's shop.

con-fed'er-a-cy, 1 kən-fed'ər-ə-sı; 2 cŏn-fĕd'er-a-çy, *n*. [*con-fed'er-a-cies,* pl.] **1.** A number of states or persons in league with one another; league; confederation; as the League of Nations. **2.** [**Confederacy**] The alliance of the Southern States of the United States at the time of the War Between the States; the **Confederate States of America.**

con-fed'er-ate, 1 kən-fed'ər-ēt; 2 cŏn-fĕd'er-āt, *vt*. & *vi*. [*con'fed-er-at"ed; con-fed'er-at"ing.*] To form a confederacy.

con-fed'er-ate, 1 kən-fed'ər-ət; 2 cŏn-fĕd'er-at. **I.** *a*. Associated in a confederacy; as, the *Confederate* States. **II.** *n*. **1.** One who is united with another in a league or plot; an associate; accomplice. **2.** [**Confederate**] A member of the Confederate army or one who supported the Confederacy.

con-fed"er-a'tion, 1 kən-fed"ər-ē'shən; 2 cŏn-fĕd"er-ā'shon, *n*. **1.** The act of becoming allied together. **2.** A confederacy

con-fer', 1 kən-fūr'; 2 cŏn-fẽr', *v*. [*con-ferred'; con-fer'ring.*] **I.** *t*. To grant as a gift or benefit; bestow; as, to *confer* diplomas. **II.** *i*. To hold a discussion; consult. — **con-fer'ment,** *n*. — **con-fer'rer,** *n*.
SYN.: consider, deliberate, give, impart, offer.

con'fer-ence, 1 kən'fər-ens; 2 cŏn'fer-ĕnç, *n*. **1.** A meeting held to discuss plans or give advice, etc.; an official council. **2.** Conversation; discourse.

con-fess', 1 kən-fes'; 2 cŏn-fĕs', *v*. [*con-fessed'* or *con-fest'; con-fess'ing.*] **I.** *t*. **1.** To admit, concede, or acknowledge (one's guilt); own; avow. **2.** To acknowledge belief in, as a doctrine. **3.** To demonstrate; disclose; reveal. **4.** To present the confession of, as to a priest; as, she *confessed* herself. **5.** To hear the confession of. **II.** *i*. **1.** To make acknowledgment, as of fault, crime or error. **2.** To make confession to a priest. — **con-fess'ed-ly,** *adv*. By confession.

con-fes'sion, 1 kən-fesh'ən; 2 cŏn-fĕsh'-on, *n*. **1.** The act of telling one's faults; avowal; acknowledgment. **2.** That which is confessed; a creed. — **con-fes'sion-al,** *n*. In the Roman Catholic Church, a priest's cabinet for hearing confessions.

con-fes'sor, 1 kən-fes'ər; 2 cŏn-fĕs'or, *n*. **1.** One who acknowledges his faith in Christianity, especially in the face of persecution. **2.** In the Roman Catholic Church, one who goes to confession. **3.** A priest who hears confessions. **con-fes'ser** ‡.

con-fet'ti, 1 kən-fet'ı; 2 cŏn-fĕt'i, *n. pl.*

Small pieces of brightly colored paper thrown by revelers.

con"fi-dant', 1 kən"fi-dant' or kən'fi-dant; 2 cŏn"fi-dånt' or cŏn'fi-dånt, *n*. A person to whom secrets are entrusted. — **con"fi-dante',** *n. feminine.*

con-fide', 1 kən-faid'; 2 cŏn-fīd', *v*. [*con-fid'ed; con-fid'ing.*] **I.** *t*. To reveal in trust, or confidence; entrust (to). **II.** *i*. To repose confidence (in). — **con-fid'er,** *n*. — **con-fid'-ing,** *pa*. — **con-fid'ing-ly,** *adv*.

con'fi-dence, 1 kən'fi-dens; 2 cŏn'fi-dĕnç, *n*. **1.** Trust in or reliance upon another; belief in a person or thing; as, *confidence* in one's parents. **2.** Assurance; self-reliance; as, *confidence* in one's ability. **3.** Private conversation or communication; a secret; as, to exchange *confidences.*

con'fi-dent, 1 kən'fi-dent; 2 cŏn'fi-dĕnt, *a*. Having confidence; self-reliant; as, a *confident* speaker. — **con'fi-dent-ly,** *adv*.

con"fi-den'tial, 1 kən"fi-den'shəl; 2 cŏn"fi-dĕn'shal, *a*. **1.** Enjoying the confidence of another; trusted with private affairs or secrets; intimate; as, *confidential* associates. **2.** Given in confidence; secret. — **con"fi-den'tial-ly,** *adv*.

con-fig"ur-a'tion, 1 kən-fig"yur-ē'-shən; 2 cŏn-fĭg"yur-ā'shon, *n*. The outline of something; structural arrangement.

con-fine', 1 kən-fain'; 2 cŏn-fīn', *vt*. [*con-fined'; con-fin'ing.*] **1.** To shut up within an enclosure; imprison; limit; restrict. **2.** To oblige to stay indoors. — **con-fine'ment,** *n*.

con'fine, 1 kən'fain; 2 cŏn'fīn, *n*. That which forms a boundary; limit; border.

con-firm', 1 kən-fūrm'; 2 cŏn-fīrm', *vt*. **1.** To make certain of the correctness of; corroborate; verify; as, to *confirm* a report. **2.** To strengthen; as, to *confirm* faith. **3.** To approve; ratify; sanction. **4.** In religion, to receive into the church. — **con-firm'a-ble,** *a*.
SYN.: assure, establish, fix, uphold.

con"fir-ma'tion, 1 kən"fər-mē'shən; 2 cŏn"fīr-mā'shon, *n*. **1.** The act of confirming. **2.** That which confirms; proof. **3.** The rite after baptism of full admission into certain churches. — **con-firm'a-tive** *a*.

con-firmed', 1 kən-fūrmd'; 2 cŏn-fîrmd', *pa*. Fixed; firmly established; inveterate, as, a *confirmed* drunkard.

con'fis-cate, 1 kən'fis-kēt or kən-fis'kēt; 2 cŏn'fis-ēāt or cŏn-fĭs'ēāt, *vt*. [*con'fis-cat"-ed; con'fis-cat"ing.*] To take according to law, as forfeited to the public use or treasury; as, to *confiscate* liquor. — **con"fis-ca'-tion,** *n*. — **con'fis-ca"tor,** *n*. — **con-fis'ca-to-ry,** *a*.

con"fla-gra'tion, 1 kən"flə-grē'shən; 2 cŏn"fla-grā'shon, *n*. A great fire.

con-flict', 1 kən-flikt'; 2 cŏn-flĭet', *vi*. To come into collision, be in mutual opposition; clash; contend. — **con-flict'ing,** *a*.

1: ə = final; ı = habit; aisle; au = out; oil; iū = feud; chin; go; H = loch; ŋ = sing; thin, this.
2: wǫlf, dǫ; bŏŏk, bōōt; fųll, rųle, cūre, bŭt, bûrn; ŏil; c = k; ġo, ġem; iŋk; ç = s; thin, this.

con'flict, 1 kŏn'flĭkt; 2 cŏn'flĭet, *n.* A contest; strife; as, war is a useless *conflict*.

con'flu-ence, 1 kŏn'flu-ens; 2 cŏn'flu̇-ĕnç, *n.* A joining of streams and the point where they join; a union. —**con'flu-ent,** *a.*

con'flux, 1 kŏn'flŭks; 2 cŏn'flŭks, *n.* Same as *confluence*.

con-form', 1 kŏn-fōrm'; 2 cŏn-fôrm', *v.* **I.** *t.* To make like in form: with *to;* as, to *conform* conduct *to* a rule. **II.** *i.* To act in accord; correspond; comply. —**con-form'-a-ble,** *a.* — **con-form'a-bly,** *adv.* — **con-form'ist,** *n.* **con-form'er** ‡.

con″for-ma'tion, 1 kŏn″fōr-mē'shăn; 2 cŏn″fôr-mā'shon, *n.* **1.** The manner of formation of a body; general structure, form, or outline. **2.** The act of conforming, adapting, or causing to conform. **3.** The assuming of form in an object by the development of its parts.

con-form'i-ty, 1 kŏn-fōrm'ĭ-tĭ; 2 cŏn-fôrm'i-ty, *n.* [*con-form'i-ties,* pl.] **1.** Likeness in form, manner, or use. **2.** Agreement; acquiescence.

con-found', 1 kŏn-faund'; 2 cŏn-found', *vt.* **1.** To strike with confusion or amazement; perplex; overwhelm; abash; as, the accusation *confounded* him. **2.** To confuse with something else; mix; as, to *confound* means with end. —**con-found'ed,** *a.*

con-front', 1 kŏn-frŭnt'; 2 cŏn-frŏnt', *vt.* **1.** To stand face to face with; face defiantly; as, to *confront* one's enemy. **2.** To put face to face.

Con-fu'cius, 1 kŏn-fiū'shŭs; 2 cŏn-fū'-shŭs, *n.* (551-478 B.C.), Chinese sage, founder of **Con-fu'cian-ism,** a system of ethical and philosophical teachings upon which Chinese law and education were based. —**Con-fu'cian,** *a.* & *n.*

con-fuse', 1 kŏn-fiūz'; 2 cŏn-fū̱ẕ', *vt.* [*con-fused'; con-fus'ing.*] **1.** To perplex or perturb the mind of; bewilder; abash; disconcert; as, the traffic *confused* him. **2.** To mix indiscriminately; disorder; derange; as, to *confuse* the colors of a picture. — **con-fus'ed-ly,** *adv.* —**con-fus'ed-ness,** *n.*

con-fu'sion, 1 kŏn-fiū'zhăn; 2 cŏn-fū' zhon, *n.* The act of confusing, or the state of being confused; perplexity; distraction; turmoil; embarrassment; shame.

con-fute', 1 kŏn-fiūt'; 2 cŏn-fūt', *vt.* [*con-fut'ed; con-fut'ing.*] **1.** To prove to be false or invalid; refute successfully. **2.** To prove (a person) to be in the wrong; as, to *confute* one's critics. —**con″fu-ta'tion,** *n.* —**con-fut'er,** *n.*

Cong. Abbreviation of *Congregation, Congregational, Congress, Congressional.*

con-geal', 1 kŏn-jĭl'; 2 cŏn-ġēl', *vt.* & *vi.* To convert or be converted from a fluid to a solid condition; coagulate; stiffen; harden; freeze. —**con-geal'a-ble,** *a.*

con-ge'nial, 1 kŏn-jīn'yəl; 2 cŏn-ġēn'-yal, *a.* **1.** Having similar character or tastes; sympathetic; as, *congenial* friends. **2.** Suited to one's disposition; agreeable. — **con-ge″ni-al'i-ty,** *n.* — **con-ge'nial-ly,** *adv.*

con-gen'i-tal, 1 kŏn-jen'ĭ-təl; 2 cŏn-ġĕn'i-tal, *a.* Born with; existing from birth; as, a *congenital* defect. —**con-gen'i-tal-ly,** *adv.*

con'ger=eel″, 1 kŏŋ'ger-īl″; 2 cŏn'ġer̠-ēl″, *n.* A marine eel from 4 to 10 feet long.

con-gest', 1 kŏn-jest'; 2 cŏn-ġĕst', *v.* **I.** *t.* **1.** To collect or crowd together, overcrowd; as, to *congest* the city's streets. **2.** In medicine, to overload an organ with blood. **II.** *i.* To become congested. —**con-gest'ed,** *a.* —**con-ges'tion,** *n.*

con-glom'er-ate, 1 kŏn-glŏm'ər-ēt; 2 cŏn-ḡlŏm'er-āt, *vt.* & *vi.* [*con-glom'er-at″ed; con-glom'er-at″ing.*] To gather into a cohering mass. —**con-glom″er-a'tion,** *n.*

con-glom'er-ate, 1 kŏn-glŏm'ər-ĭt; 2 cŏn-ḡlŏm'er-at. **I.** *a.* Massed or clustered; consisting of loosely cemented materials of various kind; as, *conglomerate* clay. **II.** *n.* A varied collection; a rock composed of pebbles loosely cemented together.

Con'go, 1 kŏŋ'go; 2 cŏn̠'ḡo, *n.* A river of west Africa flowing 3,000 miles from Lake Nyassa region to the South Atlantic Ocean. —**Belgian Congo,** a Belgian colony in central west Africa. —**French Congo,** a country in west Africa; now officially called *French Equatorial Africa.*

Congo Free State. The former name of *Belgian Congo.*

con-grat'u-late, 1 kŏn-grăch'u-[*or* grat'-yu-]lēt; 2 cŏn-ḡrăch'u-[*or* ḡrăt'yu̱-]lāt, *vt.* [*con-grat'u-lat″ed; con-grat'u-lat″ing.*] To express sympathetic pleasure in the joy or good fortune of another. —**con-grat″u-la'-tion,** *n.* — **con-grat'u-la″tor,** *n.* — **con-grat'u-la-to-ry,** *a.*

con'gre-gate, 1 kŏn'grĭ-gēt; 2 cŏn'ḡre-ḡāt, *vt.* & *vi.* [*con'gre-gat″ed; con'gre-gat″-ing.*] To bring or come together into a crowd; assemble; as, to *congregate* in a hall.

con″gre-ga'tion, 1 kŏn″grĭ-gē'shăn; 2 cŏn″ḡre-ḡā'shon, *n.* **1.** The act of congregating. **2.** An assemblage, as at church; a religious community or communion.

con″gre-ga'tion-al, 1 kŏn″grĭ-gē'-shăn-əl; 2 cŏn″ḡre-ḡā'shon-al, *a.* **1.** Pertaining to a congregation. **2.** [**Congregational**] Pertaining to Congregationalism or to the Congregationalists.

con″gre-ga'tion-al-ism, 1 kŏn″grĭ-gē'shăn-əl-izm; 2 cŏn″ḡre-ḡā'shon-al-i̱sm, *n.* The method of church government that makes the authority of the local congregation supreme within its own domain, or [**Congregationalism**] the religious denom-

ination founded on that method. — **Con″-
gre-ga′tion-al-ist,** *n.*

con′gress, 1 kon′gres; 2 cŏn′grĕs, *n.* **1.**
An assembly or conference. **2.** [**Congress**]
The national law-making body of the
United States. **3.** A coming together; inter-
course. — **con-gres′sion-al,** *a.*

Con′gress-man, 1 kon′gres-mən; 2
cŏn′grĕs-man, *n.* [**Con′gress-men,** pl.] A
member of the United States Congress,
particularly of the House of Representatives. — **Con′gress-wo″man,** *n.*

con′gru-ent, 1 kon′gru-ent; 2 cŏn′grụ-
ĕnt, *a.* Having joint or common agreement or conformity. — **con′gru-ence,** *n.*
con′gru-en-cy ‡. — **con′gru-ent-ly,** *adv.*

con′gru-ous, 1 kon′gru-us; 2 cŏn′grụ-
ŭs, *a.* Harmoniously related or combined;
appropriate. — **con′gru-ous-ly,** *adv.*

con′ic, 1 kon′ĭk; 2 cŏn′ie, *a.* Cone-shaped.
con′i-cal ‡.

con′i-fer, 1 kon′ĭ-fər; 2 cŏn′i-fer, *n.* A
cone-bearing plant of the pine family. —
co-nif′er-ous, *a.*

conj. Abbreviation of *conjunction.*

con-jec′ture, 1 kon-jek′chur *or* -tiur;
2 cŏn-jĕe′chụr *or* -tūr. **I.** *vt.* & *vi.* [*con-
jec′tured; con-jec′tur-ing.*] To judge from
incomplete evidence; surmise; guess. **II.**
n. **1.** An indecisive opinion; guess; surmise. **2.** The act of conjecturing. — **con-
jec′tur-al-ly,** *adv.* — **con-jec′tur-al,** *a.* —
con-jec′tur-er, *n.*

con-join′, 1 kon-join′; 2 cŏn-jŏin′, *vt.* &
vi. To join together; connect; unite.

con-joint′, 1 kon-joint′; 2 cŏn-jŏint′, *a.*
Associated; conjoined. — **con-joint′ly,** *adv.*

con′ju-gal, 1 kon′ju-gəl; 2 cŏn′jụ-ḡal, *a.*
Pertaining to marriage; matrimonial. —
con′ju-gal-ly, *adv.* — **con″ju-gal′i-ty,** *n.*

con′ju-gate, 1 kon′ju-gēt; 2 cŏn′jụ-ḡāt,
vt. [*con′ju-gat″ed; con′ju-gat″ing.*] To give
in order the forms of: said of verbs.

con″ju-ga′tion, 1 kon″ju-gē′shən; 2
cŏn″jụ-ḡā′shon, *n.* In grammar, the act of
giving the forms of a verb in order.

con-junc′tion, 1 kon-jụŋk′shən; 2 cŏn-
jụ̣ŋe′shon, *n.* **1.** The state of being joined
together. **2.** A part of speech that connects
words, clauses, and sentences. **3.** In as-
tronomy, the nearest apparent approach
of two heavenly bodies to each other. —
con-junc′tive, *a.* — **con-junc′tive-ly,** *adv.*

con′jure[1], 1 kun′jər *or* kon′jər; 2 cŏn′jur
or cŏn′jur, *v.* [*con′jured; con′jur-ing.*] **I.** *t.*
1. To bring about by magical means. **2.** To
summon, drive away, or control by magical
art; as, to *conjure* evil spirits. **II.** *i.* To
practise magic; use magical charms;
also, to juggle. — **con″ju-ra′tion,** *n.* — **con′-
jur-er**[1], *n.* **con′jur-or**[1]‡.

con-jure′[2], 1 kon-jūr′; 2 cŏn-jụr′, *v.*

[*con-jured′; con-jur′-ing.*] **I.** *t.* To call on
in the name of God or of something
sacred; appeal to solemnly. **II.** *i.* To bind
oneself by oath taken with others. — **con″-
jur-a′tion,** *n.* — **con-jur′er**[2], *n.* **con-jur′-
or**[2]‡.

Conn. Abbreviation of *Connecticut* (official).

con-nect′, 1 kə-nekt′; 2 cŏ-nĕet′, *vt.* &
vi. **1.** To set or bring together; join; unite
or combine; associate or be associated. **2.**
To be in close relation. — **con-nect′ed,** *a.*
— **con-nect′ed-ly,** *adv.* — **con-nec′tor,** *n.*
SYN.: attach, engage, fasten, relate.

Con-nect′i-cut, 1 kə-net′ı-kut; 2 cŏ-
nĕt′i-kŭt, *n.* A northeastern State of the
United States (4,820 square miles); capital, Hartford.

con-nec′tion, 1 kə-nek′shən; 2 cŏ-nĕe′-
shon, *n.* **1.** The act of connecting or the
state of being connected; union; combination. **2.** Family relationship; a relative.
3. A body of persons connected by relationship, belief, dealings, etc., or any
member of such a group. **4.** That which
connects or serves as a bond of union. **5.** A
direct transfer from one route to another,
as in railway service.

con-nec′tive, 1 kə-nek′tıv; 2 cŏ-nĕe′tiv.
I. *a.* Capable of connecting, or serving to
connect; causing or involving connection.
II. *n.* That which connects one thing to
another. — **con-nec′tive-ly,** *adv.*

con-nive′, 1 kə-naiv′; 2 cŏ-nīv′, *vi.*
[*con-nived′; con-niv′ing.*] **1.** To encourage
or assent to a wrong by silence or pretended ignorance: followed by *at;* as, to
connive at cruelty. **2.** To have a secret understanding; to be in collusion: followed
by *with;* as, to *connive with* a criminal.
— **con-ni′vance,** *n.* — **con-niv′er,** *n.*

con″nois-seur′, 1 kon″ı-sūr′; 2 cŏn″i-
sûr′, *n.* An able critic or judge of art, etc.

con-note′, 1 kə-nōt′; 2 cŏ-nōt′, *vt.* [*con-
not′ed; con-not′ing.*] To indicate or imply
a further meaning than that belonging to
the word. **con′no-tate** ‡. — **con″no-ta′-
tion,** *n.* — **con-no′ta-tive,** *a.* — **con-no′ta-
tive-ly,** *adv.*

con-nu′bi-al, 1 kə-niū′bı-əl; 2 cŏ-nū′-
bi-al, *a.* Pertaining to matrimony; relating
to husband or wife; matrimonial; — **con-
nu″bi-al′i-ty,** *n.* — **con-nu′bi-al-ly,** *adv.*

con′quer, 1 kon′kər; 2 cŏn′ker, *v.* **I.** *t.*
1. To overcome by force or fighting; subdue; vanquish; as, to *conquer* temptation.
2. To obtain in war, or by any conflict or
struggle; as, to *conquer* a country. **II.** *i.*
To be victorious. — **con′quer-a-ble,** *a.*

con′quer-or, 1 kon′kər-ər; 2 cŏn′ker-or,
n. One who or that which conquers.

con′quest, 1 kon′kwest; 2 cŏn′kwĕst, *n.*

1: ə =final; ı =habit; aisle; au =out; øil; iū =feud; chin; go; H =loch; ŋ =sing; thin, this.
2: wǫlf, dǫ; book, boot; fụll, rụle, cūre, bŭt, bûrn; øil; e =k; ḡo, ġem; iŋk; ç =s; thin, this.

1. The act of conquering; as, the *conquest* of the West. **2.** The thing conquered.

con-quis′ta-dor, 1 kən-kwis′tə-dor or (Sp.) kon-kĭs″ta-dōr′; 2 eŏn-kwĭs′ta-dôr or (Sp.) eŏn-kĭs″tä-dôr′, *n.* A Spanish conqueror of Indian empires in America.

con″san-guin′i-ty, 1 kən″san-gwin′-ɪ-tɪ; 2 eŏn″săn-ḡwĭn′i-ty, *n.* Blood‐relationship.

con′science, 1 kən′śhens; 2 eŏn′shĕnç, *n.* The ability to make decisions as to right and wrong; moral sense. **—con′-science-less,** *a.*

con″sci-en′tious, 1 kən″śhɪ-[or -sɪ-]en′śhus; 2 eŏn″shi-[or -si-]ĕn′shŭs, *a.* Governed or dictated by conscience; obedient to the dictates of conscience; as, a *conscientious* workman.—**con″sci-en′tious-ly,** *adv.* **—con″sci-en′tious-ness,** *n.*

con′scious, 1 kən′śhus; 2 eŏn′shŭs, *a.* **1.** Having such knowledge as is conveyed by immediate sensation or perception; as, a *conscious* act. **2.** Embarrassed by the sense of one's own individuality and the observation of others. **3.** Cognizant; aware; as, *conscious* of the stares of those about him. **4.** Present to the mind; recognized as belonging to oneself; as, *conscious* superiority. **—con′scious-ly,** *adv.* **—con′scious-ness,** *n.*

con-script′, 1 kən-skript′; 2 eŏn-serĭpt′, *vt.* To force into military service; draft. **—con-scrip′tion,** *n.*

con′script, 1 kən′skript; 2 eŏn′serĭpt. **I.** *a.* Registered; enrolled; as, a *conscript* army. **II.** *n.* One who is forcibly enrolled for military service.

con′se-crate, 1 kən′sɪ-krēt; 2 eŏn′se-erāt, *vt.* [con′se-crat″ed; con′se-crat″ing.] **1.** To set apart for sacred use; as, to *consecrate* a church. **2.** To dedicate; as, to *consecrate* one's life to a cause. **3.** To make reverend; hallow. **—con″se-cra′tion,** *n.*

con-sec′u-tive, 1 kən-sek′yu-tɪv; 2 eŏn-sĕe′yu̬-tiv, *a.* **1.** Following in unbroken succession; successive; as, the months of the year are *consecutive*. **2.** Consequent: with *to*. **— con-sec′u-tive-ly,** *adv.* **— con-sec′u-tive-ness,** *n.*

con-sen′sus, 1 kən-sen′sus; 2 eŏn-sĕn′-sŭs, *n.* A collective opinion; general agreement.

con-sent′, 1 kən-sent′; 2 eŏn-sĕnt′. **I.** *vi.* To yield willingly; accede, as to a request; as, he *consented* to the operation. **II.** *n.* **1.** A voluntary yielding to what is proposed or desired by another; compliance. **2.** Agreement; accord. **— con-sen′tient,** *a.* Mutually agreeing; consonant.

SYN.: acquiesce, agree, allow, comply.

con′se-quence, 1 kən′sɪ-kwens; 2 eŏn′-se-kwĕnç, *n.* **1.** That which follows as a result or conclusion; as, his death was the consequence of his dangerous actions. **2.** Distinguishing quality; superior ability; importance; as, a man of *consequence*.

con′se-quent, 1 kən′sɪ-kwent; 2 eŏn′-se-kwĕnt. **I.** *a.* Following as a natural result or as a logical conclusion; logical; as, excitement and *consequent* confusion. **II.** *n.* The conclusion of an inference; a development which follows another. **— con′se-quent-ly,** *adv.*

con″se-quen′tial, 1 kən″sɪ-kwen′śhəl; 2 eŏn″se-kwĕn′shal, *a.* **1.** Having or showing importance; self‐important. **2.** Following logically; consequent.

con″ser-va′tion, 1 kən″sər-vē′śhən; 2 eŏn″ser-vā′shon, *n.* The act of keeping from loss, decay, etc.; also, the preservation of natural resources; as, the *conservation* of the soil. **— con″ser-va′tion-ist,** *n.*

con-ser′va-tive, 1 kən-sûr′və-tɪv; 2 eŏn-sẽr′va-tiv. **I.** *a.* **1.** Adhering to the existing order of things; opposed to change or progress; as, the *conservative* element of a city; a *conservative* thinker. **2.** Conserving; preserving; **3.** Not extreme; moderate; safe; as, a *conservative* estimate. **4.** [**Conservative**] Belonging to or characteristic of a party opposed to radical reform measures. **II.** *n.* **1.** A conservative person. **2.** [**Conservative**] A member of a Conservative party. **— con-ser′va-tism** or **Con-ser′-va-tism,** *n.* **— con-ser′va-tive-ly,** *adv.*

con-ser′va-to-ry, 1 kən-sûr′və-to-rɪ; 2 eŏn-sẽr′va-to-ry, **I.** *a.* Adapted or intended to preserve; as, a *conservatory* measure. **II.** *n.* [con-ser′va-to-ries, pl.] **1.** A building covered with glass for the protection of tender plants; a greenhouse. **2.** A school of art or science; as, a *conservatory* of music.

con-serve′, 1 kən-sûrv′; 2 eŏn-sẽrv′, *vt.* [con-served′; con-serv′ing.] **1.** To keep from loss, decay, or injury; supervise and protect. **2.** To preserve with sugar, as fruits. **— con-serv′a-ble,** *a.* **— con′ser-va″tor,** *n.*

con′serve, 1 kən′sûrv; 2 eŏn′sẽrv, *n.* A sweetmeat in which fruits, etc., are preserved in sugar. **con′serves** ‡.

con-sid′er, 1 kən-sid′ər; 2 eŏn-sĭd′er, *v.* **I.** *t.* **1.** To reflect upon; give close attention to; ponder; as, to *consider* a matter before deciding. **2.** To think to be; estimate; as, to *consider* it wrong. **3.** To think well of; treat well; as, to be highly *considered* by one's townsmen. **4.** To make allowance for; as, *considering* their lack of training, they do well. **5.** To tip; fee; remunerate; as, you must *consider* the porter. **6.** To be of the opinion (that): ·followed by a clause as object; as, he *considers* that he has not been well treated. **II.** *i.* To think closely; deliberate.

SYN.: esteem, examine, study, weigh.

con-sid′er-a-ble, 1 kən-sid′ər-ə-bl; 2 ĕŏn-sĭd′er-a-bl, *a.* **1.** Somewhat large in amount, extent, etc. **2.** Of noteworthy size or importance. **—con-sid′er-a-bly,** *adv.*

con-sid′er-ate, 1 kən-sid′ər-ıt; 2 ĕŏn-sĭd′er-at, *a.* Showing or given to consideration; thoughtful; kind. **—con-sid′er-ate-ly,** *adv.* **—con-sid′er-ate-ness,** *n.*

con-sid″er-a′tion, 1 kən-sid″ər-ē′shən; 2 ĕŏn-sĭd″er-ā′shon, *n.* **1.** The act of considering; as, after long *consideration*, he declined. **2.** Thoughtful and kindly feeling or treatment; as, he showed *consideration* for the girl in her sorrow. **3.** A circumstance to be taken into account. **4.** Something given in return for a service; remuneration. **5.** Importance; consequence.

con-sid′er-ing, 1 kən-sid′ər-ıŋ; 2 ĕŏn-sĭd′er-ing, *prep.* In view of.

con-sign′, 1 kən-sain′; 2 ĕŏn-sīn′, *vt.* **1.** To deliver into the care and control of another; entrust; commit; transfer; as, he *consigned* the package to his friend. **2.** In commerce, to forward or deliver to another to be sold, disposed of, etc., as merchandise. **—con-sign′ment,** *n.*

con″sign-ee′, 1 kən″sain-ī′; 2 ĕŏn″sīn-ē′, *n.* In commerce, a person to whom property has been consigned.

con-sign′or, 1 kən-sain′ər *or* kən″sı-nēr′; 2 ĕŏn-sī′nor *or* ĕŏn″si-nôr′, *n.* One who consigns. **con-sign′er** ‡.

con-sist′, 1 kən-sist′; 2 ĕŏn-sĭst′, *vi.* **1.** To be composed; be made up: followed by *of;* as, man *consists of* soul and body. **2.** To have as its foundation, substance, or nature; be: followed by *in;* as, true charity does not *consist in* almsgiving.

con-sis′ten-cy, 1 kən-sis′ten-sı; 2 ĕŏn-sĭs′tĕn-çy, *n.* [*con-sis′ten-cies,* pl.] **1.** A state of agreement or harmony between things, acts, or statements; as, the *consistency* of the acts of a person with one another. **2.** Degree of firmness or density; as, the *consistency* of butter. **con-sis′tence** ‡. **con-sis′tent,** *a.* **—con-sis′tent-ly,** *adv.*

con-sis′to-ry, 1 kən-sis′to-rı *or* kən′sıs-tə-rı; 2 ĕŏn-sĭs′to-ry *or* ĕŏn′sis-te-ry, *n.* [*con-sis′to-ries,* pl.] A church court; also the place where it is held.

con″so-la′tion, 1 kən″so-lē′shən; 2 ĕŏn″so-lā′shon, *n.* **1.** The act of comforting or the state of being comforted. **2.** A comforting thought or fact.

con-sol′a-to-ry, 1 kən-sŏl′ə-to-rı; 2 ĕŏn-sol′a-to-ry. *a.* Tending to console.

con-sole′, 1 kən-sōl′; 2 ĕŏn-sōl′, *vt.* [*con-soled′; con-sol′ing.*] To comfort (a person) in grief or sorrow; solace; cheer. **—con-sol′a-ble,** *a.* **—con-sol′ing,** *pa.*

con′sole, 1 kən′sōl; 2 ĕŏn′sōl, *n.* **1.** A console=table or a radio cabinet modeled after a console=table. **2.** That part of an

organ containing the manuals and stops. **—con′sole=ta″ble,** *n.* A table supported wholly or in part by brackets.

con-sol′i-date, 1 kən-səl′ı-dēt; 2 ĕŏn-sŏl′i-dāt, *v.* [*con-sol′i-dat″ed; con-sol′i-dat″-ing.*] **I.** *t.* To make solid, firm, coherent, or united; as, to *consolidate* the forces of an army. **II.** *i.* To become united or solid. **—con-sol″i-da′tion,** *n.*

con″som-mé′, 1 kĕn̄″so-mē′; 2 ĕŏn̄″so-me′, *n.* Clear meat=soup.

con′so-nance, 1 kən′so-nəns; 2 ĕŏn′so-nanç, *n.* Agreement, as of sounds; accord; concord. **con′so-nan-cy** ‡.

con′so-nant, 1 kən′so-nənt; 2 ĕŏn so-nant. *n.* An alphabetic sound not easily uttered without a vowel; a letter representing such a sound; as, *h, k, m, n,* and *t* are *consonants.* **—con″so-nan′tal,** *a.* **—con′so-nant-ness,** *n.*

con-sort′, 1 kən-sērt′; 2 ĕŏn-sôrt′, *v.* **I.** *t.* To join; associate; as, *consort* yourself with honest men. **II.** *ı.* To keep company.

con′sort, 1 kən′sērt; 2 ĕŏn′sôrt, *n.* **1.** A companion or associate; a husband or wife; as, the *consort* of a king. **2.** An accompanying vessel; as, the ship's *consort.*

con-spic′u-ous, 1 kən-spik′yu-ʊs; 2 ĕŏn-spĭe′yu̧-ŭs, *a.* **1.** Clearly visible; prominent; obvious; striking; as, he was *conspicuous* for his height. **2.** Eminent; notable; as, *conspicuous* for bravery. **—con-spic′u-ous-ly,** *adv.* **—con-spic′u-ous-ness,** *n.*

con-spir′a-cy, 1 kən-spır′ə-sı; 2 ĕŏn-spīr′a-çy; *n.* [*con-spir′a-cies,* pl.] A secret combination for an evil purpose; plot; also, any combination to surprize.

con-spir′a-tor, 1 kən-spır′ə-tər *or* -tər; 2 ĕŏn-spīr′a-tor, *n.* One who conspires.

con-spire′, 1 kən-spair′; 2 ĕŏn-spīr′, *v.* [*con-spired′; con-spir′ing.*] **I.** *t.* To plot; scheme for; as, to *conspire* one's death. **II.** *i.* **1.** To join in or form an unlawful plot; as, to *conspire* against the government. **2.** To concur in action or endeavors, as circumstances, agencies, or persons; as, everything *conspired* against us.

con′sta-ble, 1 kən′stə-bl *or* kun′stə-bl; 2 ĕŏn′sta-bl *or* eŏn′sta-bl, *n.* **1.** An officer of the peace; a policeman. **2.** A high military officer in medieval monarchies.

con-stab′u-la-ry, 1 kən-stab′yu-lā-rı; 2 ĕŏn-stăb′yu̧-lâ-ry. *n.* [*con-stab′u-la′ries,* pl.] Constables collectively; a military police force.

con′stan-cy, 1 kən′stən-sı; 2 ĕŏn′-stan-çy, *n.* **1.** Steadiness in purpose or action; faithfulness. **2.** Stability.
SYN.: devotion, fidelity, loyalty, perseverance.

con′stant, 1 kən′stənt; 2 ĕŏn′stant. **I.** *a.* **1.** Steady in purpose; resolute; persevering; faithful; as, *constant* in his resolve to reform. **2.** Steady in movement; long= continuing, or continually recurring; in-

1: ə =final; ı =habit; aisle; au =out; eil; iu =feud; ehin; go; H =loch; ŋ =sing; thin, this.
2: wolf, do; book, boot; full, rule, cure, bŭt, bûrn; ŏil; e =k; ḡo, gem; iṇk; ç =s; thin, this.

variable; as, *constant* rains. **II.** *n.* An unchanging quality. — **con'stant-ly**, *adv.*

con″stel-la′tion, 1 kən″ste-lē′shən; 2 cŏn″stĕ-lā′shon, *n.* A group or cluster of stars, or a region of the sky occupied by such a group.

con″ster-na′tion, 1 kən″stər-nē′shən; 2 cŏn″ster-nā′shon, *n.* Sudden overwhelming fear; terror with confusion; dismay.

con″sti-pa′tion, 1 kən″stɪ-pē′shən; 2 cŏn″sti-pā′shon, *n.* A condition of the bowels marked by infrequent and irregular movements. — **con'sti-pat″ed**, *a.*

con-stit′u-en-cy, 1 kən-stit′yu-en-sɪ; 2 cŏn-stĭt′yụ-ĕn-çy, *n.* [*con-stit′u-en-cies*, pl.] A body of constituents.

con-stit′u-ent, 1 kən-stit′yu-ent; 2 cŏn-stĭt′yụ-ĕnt. **I.** *a.* **1.** Being a necessary part; component; as, the *constituent* elements of salt. **2.** Entitled to vote for a public officer or representative; as, the *constituent* population. **II.** *n.* **1.** One part of many out of which something is made; an ingredient or element. **2.** One who constitutes or elects another; a voter; a client; as, the *constituents* of a senator.

con'sti-tute, 1 kən′stɪ-tiūt; 2 cŏn-sti-tūt, *vt.* [*con'sti-tut″ed; con'sti-tut″ing*.] **1.** To make (anything) what it is; make up; frame; compose; as, nine judges *constitute* the U. S. Supreme Court. **2.** To establish, as by authority; enact; as, they *constituted* themselves a court of law. **3.** To depute; appoint; as, I *constitute* you my spokesman.

con″sti-tu′tion, 1 kən″stɪ-tiū′shən; 2 cŏn″sti-tū′shon, *n.* **1.** The act of constituting; as, at the time of the *constitution* of the courts. **2.** A system of related parts; as, the *constitution* of salt. **3.** Composition or make-up; bodily frame or temperament; as, he has a poor *constitution*. **4.** The fundamental or organic law of a state or of an association; especially [**Constitution**], that of the United States of America.

con″sti-tu″tion-al, 1 kən″stɪ-tiū′shən-əl; 2 cŏn″sti-tū′shon-al. **I.** *a.* **1.** Pertaining to, inherent in, or affecting the constitution of a person or of a state; consistent with the constitution of a state; lawful; as, a *constitutional* amendment. **2.** Acting under and controlled by a constitution. **II.** *n.* Anything done for the benefit of one's health. — **con″sti-tu′tion-al-ly**, *adv.*

con″sti-tu″tion-al′i-ty, 1 kən″stɪ-tiū″shən-al′ɪ-tɪ; 2 cŏn″sti-tū″shon-ăl′i-ty, *n.* Accordance with a constitution.

con-strain′, 1 kən-strēn′; 2 cŏn-strān′, *vt.* **1.** To compel by physical or moral force; urge; as, hunger *constrained* him to eat. **2.** To confine by force or unnaturally.

con-straint′, 1 kən-strēnt′; 2 cŏn-strānt′, *n.* **1.** The act of forcing or state of being forced; compulsion; as, he signed

the will under *constraint*. **2.** Embarrassment. **3.** A holding back of one's natural feelings; as, to act with *constraint*.

con-strict′, 1 kən-strikt′; 2 cŏn-strĭet′, *vt.* To press into smaller space; draw together at some point; cause to cramp. — **con-stric′tor**, *n.* That which constricts; a serpent, as a boa, that crushes its prey. — **con-stric′tion**, *n.* — **con-stric′tive**, *a.*

con-struct′, 1 kən-strukt′; 2 cŏn-strŭet′, *vt.* **1.** To put together and set up; build; as, to *construct* a ship. **2.** To arrange or form in one's mind; as, to *construct* a plot. — **con-struct′er**, *n.* **con-struct′or**‡.

con-struc′tion, 1 kən-struk′shən; 2 cŏn-strŭe′shon, *n.* **1.** The act of constructing. **2.** A structure. **3.** The style of building or composing; as, the building is of steel *construction*. **4.** The act of understanding or the meaning arrived at; as, a bad *construction* was put upon his behavior. **5.** The joining of words to form a sentence. — **con-struc′tion-al**, *a.*

con-struc′tive, 1 kən-struk′tɪv; 2 cŏn-strŭe′tiv, *a.* **1.** Pertaining to construction; having power or tendency to build up; helpful; as, he made a *constructive* suggestion. **2.** Tending toward or reaching positive conclusions; as, *constructive* reasoning. — **con-struc′tive-ly**, *adv.*

con′strue, 1 kən′strū *or* kən-strū′; 2 cŏn′stru *or* cŏn-stru′, *vt. & vi.* [*con'strued; con'stru-ing*.] **1.** To state the grammatical construction of a sentence. **2.** To take to mean; interpret; as, he *construed* the remark as a compliment.

con′sul, 1 kən′sul; 2 cŏn′sŭl, *n.* **1.** An officer appointed to live in a foreign port or city to supervise his country's business interests, and to issue passports, bills of lading, certificates, etc. **2.** A chief magistrate of ancient Rome. — **con′su-lar**, *a.* Of or pertaining to a consul.

con′su-late, 1 kən′siū-lĕt; 2 cŏn-sū-lāt, *n.* **1.** The powers or term of office of a consul. **con′sul-ship**‡. **2.** The official place of business or home of a consul. **3.** Government by a consul or consuls.

con-sult′, 1 kən-sult′; 2 cŏn-sŭlt′, *v.* **I.** *t.* **1.** To ask the advice of; as, to *consult* a lawyer. **2.** To have regard to; consider; as, she *consulted* my wishes. **II.** *i.* To compare views; take counsel; confer. — **con-sul′tant**, *n.* — **con″sul-ta′tion**, *n.*

con-sume′, 1 kən-siūm′; 2 cŏn-sūm′, *vt.* [*con-sumed′; con-sum′ing*.] **1.** To demolish, as by fire; as, the flames *consumed* the house. **2.** To absorb; use up; as, he *consumed* months in writing the book. **3.** To engage completely, as interest, attention, or energy; as, rage *consumed* him.

con-sum′er, 1 kən-siūm′ər; 2 cŏn-sūm′er, *n.* One who purchases goods for his own use rather than for resale.

1: artistic, ärt; fat, fāre; fast; get, prēy; hit, polīce; obey, gō; net, ēr; full, rūle; but, bûrn;
2: ärt, āpe, făt, fâre, fȧst, sofa; mē, gĕt, prẹy, fêrn, over; hit, īce; ĭ = ē; ĩ = ē; gō, nŏt, ôr, wȯn,

con'sum-mate, 1 kən'su-mēt *or* kən-sum'ēt; 2 cŏn'sŭ-māt *or* cŏn-sŭm'āt, *vt.* [*con'sum-mat"ed; con'sum-mat"ing.*] To bring to completion or perfection; finish. —**con"sum-ma'tion,** *n.*

con-sum'mate, 1 kən-sum'ıt *or* kən'-su-mıt; 2 cŏn-sŭm'at *or* cŏn'sŭ-mat, *a.* Of the highest degree; perfect.

con-sump'tion, 1 kən-sump'shən; 2 cŏn-sŭmp'shon, *n.* **1.** The act or process of using up. **2.** A disease which causes a person to waste away; tuberculosis.

con-sump'tive, 1 kən-sump'tıv; 2 cŏn-sŭmp'tiv. **I.** *a.* **1.** Causing destruction or waste. **2.** Suffering from tuberculosis. **II.** *n.* A person affected with tuberculosis.

con'tact, 1 kən'takt; 2 cŏn'tăct, *n.* The coming together or meeting of two persons, objects, or elements.

con-ta'gion, 1 kən-tē'jən; 2 cŏn-tā'ġon, *n.* **1.** The spreading of disease from one person to another by contact, direct or indirect. **2.** The transferring of an emotional state from one to another; as, the *contagion* of his excitement. **3.** A plague.

con-ta'gious, 1 kən-tē'jus; 2 cŏn-tā'ġŭs, *a.* **1.** Spreading by contact, as a disease. **2.** Spreading disease; breeding pestilence. **3.** Causing a responsive feeling in others; as, *contagious* enthusiasm.
SYN.: communicating, infectious, pestilential.

con-tain', 1 kən-tēn'; 2 cŏn-tān', *vt.* **1.** To admit within a limited space; hold; as, the bag *contains* oranges. **2.** To comprise; consist of; include; as, a gallon *contains* four quarts. **3.** To hold in check, as an emotion; as, I could hardly *contain* my fury. **4.** To be a multiple of or exactly divisible by. —**con-tain'er,** *n.*

con-tam'i-nate, 1 kən-tam'ı-nēt; 2 cŏn-tăm'i-nāt, *vt.* [*con-tam'i-nat"ed; con-tam'i-nat"ing.*] To make impure; corrupt; spoil; as, to *contaminate* food. —**con-tam"i-na'tion,** *n.*
SYN.: defile, deprave, pollute, taint, tarnish.

con-temn', 1 kən-tem'; 2 cŏn-těm', *vt.* To despise; scorn; disregard.

con'tem-plate, 1 kən'tem-plēt *or* kən-tem'plēt; 2 cŏn'těm-plāt *or* cŏn-těm'plāt, *v.* [*con'tem-plat"ed; con'tem-plat"ing.*] **I.** *t.* **1.** To look at attentively; consider thoughtfully; as, to *contemplate* a situation. **2.** To have in mind; intend; expect. **II.** *i.* To meditate; think. —**con"tem-pla'tion,** *n.* —**con-tem'pla-tive,** *a.*

con-tem"po-ra'ne-ous, 1 kən-tem"-po-rē'nı-us; 2 cŏn-těm"po-rā'ne-ŭs, *a.* Living, happening, or existing at the same time; as, *contemporaneous* authors.

con-tem'po-ra-ry, 1 kən-tem'po-rā-rı; 2 cŏn-těm'po-râ-ry. **I.** *a.* Living or existing at the same time. **II.** *n.* [*con-tem'po-ra-ries,* pl.] A person who is contemporary.

con-tempt', 1 kən-tempt'; 2 cŏn-těmpt', *n.* **1.** Scorn or disdain, as of something despicable. **2.** Wilful disregard or open defiance of a court or a law. **3.** The state of being despised; disgrace; shame. —**con-tempt'i-ble,** *a.* —**con-tempt'i-bly,** *adv.*

con-temp'tu-ous, 1 kən-temp'chū-us *or* -tiū-us; 2 cŏn-těmp'chu̯-ŭs *or* -tū-ŭs, *a.* Disdainful; showing or expressing scorn. —**con-temp'tu-ous-ly,** *adv.*

con-tend', 1 kən-tend'; 2 cŏn-těnd', *v.* **I.** *t.* To maintain in argument; as, we *contend* that the debt should be paid. **II.** *i.* **1.** To fight to obtain or defend some object; struggle; as, to *contend* with a robber. **2.** To debate earnestly. —**con-tend'er,** *n.*
SYN.: argue, battle, combat, compete.

con-tent', 1 kən-tent'; 2 cŏn-těnt'. **I.** *vt.* To fulfil the hopes or expectations of; satisfy; as, *content* yourself with little. **II.** *a.* Satisfied; willing; as, *content* to wait. —**con-tent'ed,** *a.* Satisfied; at peace. —**con-tent'ed-ly,** *adv.* —**con-tent'ed-ness,** *n.*

con-tent'[1], *n.* Peace of mind; satisfaction; as, to be filled with *content.*

con'tent[2], 1 kən'tent *or* kən-tent'; 2 cŏn'-těnt *or* cŏn-těnt', *n.* **1.** The subject matter or train of thought treated in a piece of writing; as, the *content* of a paragraph. **2.** The things that a space or a container will hold; as, the *contents* of a basket. **3.** The capacity or measure of a container, as, the *content* of the box is a pound.

con-ten'tion, 1 kən-ten'shən; 2 cŏn-těn'shon, *n.* **1.** Strife; conflict; struggle; dispute. **2.** An object or point in an argument to be proved or defended; as, my *contention* is that the word is misused.

con-ten'tious, 1 kən-ten'shus; 2 cŏn-těn'shŭs, *a.* Quarrelsome, especially about trifles. —**con-ten'tious-ly,** *adv.* -**ness,** *n.*

con-tent'ment, 1 kən-tent'ment *or* -mənt; 2 cŏn-těnt'měnt, *n.* The state of being free from worry; satisfaction.

con-test', 1 kən-test'; 2 cŏn-těst', *vt.* **1.** To try to win; as, an army *contests* a hill; oppose; as, to *contest* an enemy advance. **2.** To dispute; oppose. —**con-tes'tant,** *n.*

con'test, 1 kən'test; 2 cŏn'těst, *n.* **1.** A struggle; fight; as, a *contest* at arms. **2.** A trial of skill; as, a boxing *contest.*
SYN.: combat, competition, conflict, dispute.

con'text, 1 kən'tekst; 2 cŏn'těkst, *n.* The parts of a spoken or written statement that go before or follow a word, sentence, or passage and help to fix its meaning.

con"ti-gu'i-ty, 1 kən"tı-giū'ı-tı; 2 cŏn"-ti-gū'i-ty, *n.* Nearness; contact.

con-tig'u-ous, 1 kən-tıg'yu-us; 2 cŏn-tĭġ'yu̯-ŭs, *a.* Touching or joining at the boundary; near. —**con-tig'u-ous-ly,** *adv.*

con'ti-nent, 1 kən'tı-nent; 2 cŏn'ti-nĕnt, *a.* Moderate; self=controlled; chaste. —con′ti-nence, *n.* —con′ti-nent=ly, *adv.*

con′ti-nent, *n.* 1. One of the six great bodies of land on the globe: **Africa, Asia, Australia, Europe, North America, South America.** 2. [**The Continent**] Europe, apart from the British Isles.

Con″ti-nen′tal, 1 kɘn″tɪ-nen′tɘl; 2 eŏn″ti-nĕn′tal. I. *a.* 1. Belonging to Europe. 2. Pertaining to the American colonies during the period of the Revolution. 3. [**continental**] Of, like, or belonging to a continent. II. *n.* 1. A person who lives in Europe. 2. An American soldier in the Revolutionary War.

con-tin′gen-cy, 1 kɘn-tin′jen-sɪ; 2 eŏn-tĭn′ǧĕn-çy, *n.* [*con-tin′gen-cies*, pl.] A possible happening; also, a chance event.

con-tin′gent, 1 kɘn-tin′jent; 2 eŏn-tĭn′ǧĕnt. I. *a.* 1. Liable, but not certain; possible. 2. Chance; unexpected; as, a *contingent* meeting. 3. Dependent; as, *contingent* on your approval. II. *n.* A group or unit representing a larger group; especially, a division of an army or navy.

con-tin′u-al, 1 kɘn-tin′yu-ɘl; 2 eŏn-tĭn′yu-al, *a.* 1. Kept going without any break or interruption. 2. Very frequent; often repeated. —con-tin′u-al-ly, *adv.*

con-tin′u-ance, 1 kɘn-tin′yu-ɘns; 2 eŏn-tĭn′yu-anç, *n.* The act or state of continuing; duration.

con-tin″u-a′tion, 1 kɘn-tin″yu-ē′shɘn; 2 eŏn-tĭn″yu-ā′shon, *n.* 1. A beginning again after an interruption. 2. The act of carrying on without a break; as, the *continuation* of a quarrel. 3. Something added after a break; as, the *continuation* of a novel in volume two.

con-tin′ue, 1 kɘn-tin′yu; 2 eŏn-tĭn′yu, *v.* [*con-tin′ued; con-tin′u-ing.*] I. *t.* To extend or prolong; as, to *continue* a road project; to *continue* work; to *continue* a story. II. *i.* 1. To be durable; last; endure; as, to *continue* through the ages. 2. To remain; abide; as, to *continue* at school. 3. To keep on; persist.

con″ti-nu′i-ty, 1 kɘn″tɪ-niū′ɪ-tɪ; 2 eŏn″ti-nū′i-ty, *n.* [*con″ti-nu′i-ties*, pl.] 1. The state or quality of being uninterrupted. 2. An uninterrupted connection in space, time, development, etc. 3. In moving pictures, the scenario. 4. In radio, the statements made by the announcer which connect the various parts of the program.

con-tin′u-ous, 1 kɘn-tin′yu-ʊs; 2 eŏn-tĭn′yu-ŭs, *a.* Connected, extended, or prolonged without a break; unbroken; uninterrupted. —con-tin′u-ous-ly, *adv.*

con-tort′, 1 kɘn-tērt′; 2 eŏn-tôrt′, *vt.* To twist violently; wrench out of shape or place. —con-tor′tion, *n.* —con-tor′tive, *a.*

con-tour′, 1 kɘn-tūr′ *or* kɘn′tūr; 2 eŏn-tūr′ *or* eŏn′tūr, *n.* 1. The outer line which traces the shape of a figure or body; outline, as of mountains, coastline, etc. 2. An outline sketch or drawing.

con′tra-, *prefix.* Against; opposite; contrary; as, *contra*diction.

con′tra-band, 1 kɘn′trɘ-band; 2 eŏn′tra-bănd. I. *a.* Forbidden; prohibited or excluded, as by law; as, *contraband* goods. II. *n.* 1. Forbidden or smuggled goods.

con-tract′, 1 kɘn-trakt′; 2 eŏn-trăet′, *v.* I. *t.* 1. To shorten by drawing together; narrow; limit; condense; as, cold *contracts* metals. 2. In grammar, to shorten, as a word, by leaving out the middle part. 3. To take or acquire; become affected with, as a disease or a habit; as, he *contracted* a cold. 4. To arrange or settle by contract; as, to *contract* a marriage. 5. To bring on oneself; incur; as, to *contract* debts. II. *i.* 1. To shrink. 2. To make a contract; as, he *contracted* to build. —con-tract′i-ble, con-trac′tile, *a.* —con-trac′tion, *n.*

con′tract, 1 kɘn′trakt; 2 eŏn′trăet, *n.* A formal or written agreement.

SYN.: arrangement, bargain, covenant.

con-trac′tor, 1 kɘn-trak′tɘr *or* -tēr; 2 eŏn-trăe′tor, *n.* 1. One of the parties to a contract. 2. One who makes estimates on work in advance, agreeing to furnish material, services, or goods for a fixed price. 3. A muscle that serves to contract.

con″tra-dict′, 1 kɘn″trɘ-dikt′; 2 eŏn″tra-dĭet′, *v.* I. *t.* 1. To deny (a statement). 2. To be inconsistent with; as, the facts *contradict* his story. II. *i.* To utter a denial; deny; object to; oppose. —con″tra-dic′tion, *n.* —con″tra-dic′ter, *n.* —con″tra-dic′to-ri-ly, *adv.* —con″tra-dic′to-ri-ness, *n.* —con″tra-dic′to-ry, *a.*

con-tral′to, 1 kɘn-tral′to *or* -trāl′to; 2 eŏn-trăl′to *or* -trāl′to, *n.* 1. The vocal part between soprano and tenor; the female voice with the lowest range. 2. A contralto singer. —con-tral′to, *a.*

con′tra-ri-wise, 1 kɘn′trā-rɪ-waiz; 2 eŏn′-trâ-ri-wīẓ, *adv.* 1. On the contrary; on the other hand. 2. In the reverse order or opposite way. 3. Contrarily; perversely.

con′tra-ry, 1 kɘn′trār-ɪ; 2 eŏn′trâr-y. I. *a.* Opposite in disposition, character, action, or direction; different; opposing; as, he had *contrary* ideas. II. *n.* [*con′tra-ries*, pl.] 1. One of two contrary things. 2. The opposite; as, it was just the *contrary.* —con′tra-ri-ly, *adv.* —con′tra-ri-ness, *n.*

con-trast′, 1 kɘn-trast′; 2 eŏn-trȧst′, *v.* I. *t.* To compare in order to show unlikeness or difference; as, to *contrast* fall with spring. II. *i.* To show obvious differences.

con′trast, 1 kɘn′trast; 2 eŏn′trȧst, *n.* 1. The difference between things shown when compared. 2. The thing that shows a difference when compared.

---

con-trib'ute, 1 kən-trib'yūt; 2 ĕŏn-trĭb'yut, *v.* [*con-trib'ut-ed; con-trib'ut-ing.*] **I.** *t.* **1.** To give (money, help) to some cause or fund; as, he *contributed* to the Red Cross. **2.** To write for a book, magazine, newspaper, etc.; as, he *contributed* an article for the encyclopedia. **II.** *i.* To have a share in effecting a result; as, these causes *contributed* to his downfall. —**con"tri-bu'tion,** *n.* —**con-trib'u-tor,** *n.* —**con-trib'u-to-ry,** *a.* **con-trib'u-tive** ‡.

con'trite, 1 kən'trait; 2 ĕŏn'trīt, *a.* Broken= hearted over sin; grief for a wrong done. — **con'trite-ly,** *adv.* —**con'trite-ness,** *n.*

con-tri'tion, 1 kən-trĭsh'ən; 2 ĕŏn-trĭsh'on, *n.* Sincere penitence.

con-triv'ance, 1 kən-trai'vəns; 2 ĕŏn-trĭ'vanç, *n.* The act of contriving; planning; that which is contrived; an invention; plan; device.

con-trive' 1 kən-traiv'; 2 ĕŏn-trīv', *vt.* & *vi.* [*con-trived'; con-triv'ing.*] To plan; devise; invent; scheme; plot; as, they *contrived* a means of escape; he *contrived* a new brake. — **con-triv'a-ble,** *a.* —**con-triv'er,** *n.*

con-trol', 1 kən-trōl'; 2 ĕŏn-trōl'. **I.** *vt.* & *vi.* [*con-trolled'; con-trol'ling.*] To exercise a directing, restraining, or governing influence over; regulate; as, to *control* a country or airplane. **II.** *n.* **1.** The act of directing or controlling; authority; as, the United States has *control* of the Panama Canal. **2.** Restraint; as, the *control* of a sharp tongue. **3.** Any of certain devices which regulate machinery.—**con-trol'la-ble,** *a.*—**con-trol'= stick",** *n.* In aviation, a lever used to direct flight.

con-trol'ler, 1 kən-trōl'ər; 2 ĕŏn-trōl'ĕr, *n.* **1.** An officer who examines and verifies accounts. **2.** One who or that which con trols. **comp-trol'ler** ‡.

con"tro-ver'sial, 1 kən"tro-vūr'shəl; 2 ĕŏn'tro-vĕr'shal, *a.* Pertaining to controversy. — **con"tro-ver'sial-ist,** *n.* —**con"tro-ver'sial-ly,** *adv.*

con'tro-ver"sy, 1 kən'tro-vūr"sɪ; 2 ĕŏn'tro-vĕr"sy, *n.* [*con'tro-ver"sies,* pl.] A dispute as to opinions; quarrel; debate.
Syn.: altercation, argument, contention.

con'tro-vert, 1 kən'tro-vūrt *or* kən"tro-vūrt'; 2 ĕŏn'tro-vĕrt *or* ĕŏn"tro-vĕrt', *vt.* To try to disprove; oppose by reasoning; confute by argument; as, to *controvert* the statements of an opponent.

con"tu-ma'cious, 1 kən"tiu-mē'shŭs; 2 ĕŏn"tū-mā'shŭs, *a.* Characterized by contumacy. — **con"tu-ma'cious-ly,** *adv.*

con'tu-ma-cy, 1 kən'tiū-mə-sɪ; 2 ĕŏn'tū-ma-çy, *n.* [*con'tu-ma-cies,* pl.] Disregard for authority; stubborn rebellion.

con'tu-me-ly, 1 kən'tiū-mɪ-lɪ; 2 ĕŏn'tū-mē-ly, *n.* [*con'tu-me-lies,* pl.] Scornful insolence. — **con"tu-me'li-ous,** *a.*

con-tu'sion, 1 kən-tiū'ʒən; 2 ĕŏn-tū'zhon, *n.* A bruise.

co-nun'drum, 1 ko-nun'drum; 2 ĕo-nŭn'drŭm, *n.* A riddle; puzzle; perplexing question or thing.

con"va-les'cent, 1 kən"və-les'sent; 2 ĕŏn"va-lĕs'çĕnt, **I.** *a.* Recovering health after sickness. **II.** *n.* One who is regaining health after sickness.—**con"va-les'cence,** *n.*

con-vene', 1 kən-vīn'; 2 ĕŏn-vēn', *v.* [*con-vened'; con-ven'ing.*] **I.** *t.* To call together; summon. **II.** *i.* To come together; assemble; as, the meeting *convened.*

con-ve'nience, 1 kən-vīn'yens; 2 ĕŏn-vēn'yĕnç, *n.* **1.** The state, time, or quality of being convenient; freedom from discomfort; suitableness; fitness; as, I will call at your *convenience.* **2.** That which gives ease or comfort: as, tractors are a *convenience.*

con-ve'nient, 1 kən-vīn'yent; 2 ĕŏn-vēn'yĕnt, *a.* **1.** Suited to a person's comfort or ease; also, timely. **2.** Handy; as, a *convenient* door. — **con-ve'nient-ly,** *adv.*

con'vent, 1 kən'vent; 2 ĕŏn'vĕnt, *n.* **1.** A group of nuns forming a religious community. **2.** The house occupied by them.

con-ven'tion, 1 kən-ven'shən; 2 ĕŏn-vĕn'shon, *n.* **1.** A formal or stated meeting of delegates or representatives from a party, group, or organization; as, a teachers' *convention.* **2.** Any widespread practise or long=established custom followed by general consent; as, a social or moral *convention.* **3.** A contract; agreement; as, a *convention* satisfactory to both sides.

con-ven'tion-al, 1 kən-ven'shən-əl; 2 ĕŏn-vĕn'shon-al, *a.* Established by convention or custom; customary; usual, also, not original; commonplace; as, a story with a *conventional* plot. — **con-ven"tion-al'i-ty,** *n.* — **con-ven'tion-al-ly,** *adv.* — **con-ven'tion-al-ism,** *n.*

con-verge', 1 kən-vūrj'; 2 ĕŏn-vĕrġ', *v.* [*con-verged'; con-verg'ing.*] **I.** *t.* To cause to direct toward a common point. **II.** *i.* To tend toward one point; come together by gradual approach; as, interest *converged* on the circus. —**con-ver'gence,** *n.* —**con-ver'gent,** *a.*

con'ver-sant, 1 kən'vər-sənt; 2 ĕŏn'ver-sant, *a.* Having an understanding of; being familiar with, through knowledge or study; as, to be *conversant* with literature.

con"ver-sa'tion, 1 kən"vər-sē'shən; 2 ĕŏn"ver-sā'shon, *n.* An exchange of thoughts by means of speech. — **con"ver-sa'tion-al,** *a.* —**con"ver-sa'tion-al-ly,** *adv.*

con-verse', 1 kən-vūrs'; 2 ĕŏn-vĕrs', *vi.* [*con-versed'; con-vers'ing.*] To speak together alternately and without ceremony.

con'verse, 1 kən'vərs; 2 ĕŏn'vers, *a.* Turned about so that two parts are inverted or put in the opposite or contrary way. —**con'verse-ly,** *adv.*

con-ver'sion, 1 ken-vūr'shən; 2 eŏn-vẽr'shon, *n.* **1.** A change from one form to another; as, the *conversion* of iron into steel. **2.** The exchange of one object or thing for another; as, the *conversion* of stocks into money. **3.** A change in one's religion or political attitude.

con-vert', 1 ken-vūrt'; 2 eŏn-vẽrt', *vt.* **1.** To change into another state, form, or substance; transform; as, to *convert* ice into water. **2.** To turn from one faith or political party to another. **3.** To change into, or exchange for, value of another form; as, to *convert* goods into cash. — **con-vert'er** or **con-vert'or,** *n.* —**con-vert'i-ble,** *a.* —**con-vert″i-bil'i-ty,** *n.*—**con-vert'i-bly,** *adv.*

con'vert, 1 kŏn'vert; 2 eŏn'vert, *n.* A person who has been converted.

con'vex, 1 kon'veks; 2 eŏn'vĕks. **I.** *a.* Curving outward like a part of a globe or of a circle; bulging out; as, *convex* glass. **II.** *n.* A convex surface or body. — **con-vex'i-ty,** *n.* —**con'vex-ly,** *adv.*

con-vey', 1 ken-vē'; 2 eŏn-ve', *vt.* **1.** To transport from one place to another; carry; transfer; as, to *convey* coal by barges. **2.** To transmit; as, the radio *conveys* messages. —**con-vey'er,** *n.* **con-vey'or** ‡.

con-vey'ance, 1 ken-vē'əns; 2 eŏn-ve'-anç. *n.* **1.** The act of conveying. **2.** That by which anything is conveyed; a vehicle.

con-vict', 1 ken-vikt'; 2 eŏn-vĭet', *vt.* To prove guilty; find guilty after a judicial trial; as, the jury *convicted* him.

con'vict, 1 ken'vikt; 2 eŏn'vĭet, *n.* **1.** One found guilty of a crime. **2.** A person undergoing punishment for a crime.

con-vic'tion, 1 ken-vik'shən; 2 eŏn-vĭe'shon, *n.* **1.** The state of being convinced or convicted. **2.** In law, the act of convicting. **3.** Fixed belief.

con-vince', 1 ken-vins'; 2 eŏn-vĭnç', *vt.* [*con-vinced'*; *con-vinc'ing.*] **1.** To satisfy by evidence; as, *convinced* of innocence. **2.** To persuade by argument; cause to believe. —**con-vinc'ing,** *a.* —**con-vinc'ing-ly,** *adv.*

con-viv'i-al, 1 ken-viv'ı-əl; 2 eŏn-vĭv'i-al, *a.* Devoted to feasting, or good fellowship in eating and drinking; jovial.

con″vo-ca'tion, 1 ken″vo-kē'shən; 2 eŏn″vo-eā'shon, *n.* **1.** The act of convoking an assembly of people. **2.** [**Convocation**] A church congress or council.

con-voke', 1 ken-vōk'; 2 eŏn-vōk', *vt.* [*con-voked'*; *con-vok'ing.*] To call together; summon, as legislators.

con″vo-lu'tion, 1 ken″vo-liū'shən; 2 eŏn″vo-lū'shon, *n.* **1.** A winding motion. **2.** The state of being coiled or folded over on itself, as one of the folds of the brain.

con-voy', 1 ken-vei'; 2 cŏn-vŏy', *vt.* To attend as an escort; accompany for protection; escort.

con'voy, 1 ken'vei; 2 eŏn'vŏy, *n.* **1.** An accompanying protection for a fleet of ships, train of wagons, etc.; an escort. **2.** That which is convoyed.

con-vulse', 1 ken-vuls'; 2 eŏn-vŭls', *vt.* [*con-vulsed'; con-vuls'ing.*] **1.** To throw into spasms, as of disease, rage, or laughter. **2.** To shake or agitate violently.

con-vul'sion, 1 ken-vul'shən; 2 eŏn-vŭl'shon, *n.* **1.** A violent spasm or jerking of the muscles, caused by disease or poisoning; a fit. **2.** A violent fit of rage or laughter. **3.** Any violent political or social upheaval; also, any natural upheaval.—**con-vul'sive,** *a.* —**con-vul'sive-ly,** *adv.*

co'ny, 1 kō'nı; 2 eō'ny, *n.* [*co'nies,* pl.] The European rabbit; also, its skin or fur. **co'ney** ‡.

coo, 1 kū; 2 eōō. **I.** *vt. & vi.* To utter in a cooing manner; utter the note of a dove; make love. **II.** *n.* A murmuring note.

cook, 1 kuk; 2 eŏŏk. **I.** *vt. & vi.* To prepare for food by heat, as in roasting, boiling, frying, etc.; do the work of a cook. **2.** Prepare something falsely; as, to *cook* up a story or report. **II.** *n.* One who prepares food for eating. —**cook'er,** *n.*

cook'er-y, 1 kuk'ər-ı; 2 eŏŏk'er-y, *n.* [*cook'er-ies,* pl.] The art of cooking.

cook'y, 1 kuk'ı; 2 eŏŏk'y, *n.* [*cook'ies,* pl.] A small sweet cake. **cook'ey** ‡; **cook'ie** ‡.

cool, 1 kūl; 2 eōōl. **I.** *vt. & vi.* **1.** To make or become colder; chill. **2.** To calm or soothe, as anger, fear, love, etc. **II.** *a.* **1.** Not hot; somewhat cold. **2.** Serving to prevent heat; as, a *cool* garment. **3.** Self=controlled; calm; as, to be *cool* in danger. **4.** Indifferent; not cordial; as, a *cool* welcome. **III.** *n.* A moderate temperature approaching cold; as, the *cool* of a breeze. —**cool'ish,** *a.* —**cool'ly,** *adv.* —**cool'ness,** *n.*

cool'er, 1 kūl'ər; 2 eōōl'er, *n.* That which cools, as a refrigerator or water cooler.

Coo'lidge, 1 kū'lij; 2 eōō'lĭdġ, *n.* **Calvin** (1872-1933), 30th president of the United States, 1923-29.

coo'lie, 1 kū'lı; 2 eōō'li, *n.* An Oriental laborer or burden=bearer. **coo'ly** ‡.

coon, 1 kūn; 2 eōōn, *n.* The raccoon.

coop, 1 kūp; 2 eōōp. **I.** *vt.* To put into a pen; confine. **II.** *n.* An enclosure for animals; as fowls or rabbits.

coo'per[1], 1 kū'pər; 2 eōō'per, *n.* One whose business it is to make barrels, casks, etc. —**coo'per-age,** *n.* The work of a cooper.

Coo'per[2], *n.* **James Fenimore** (1789-1851), American novelist; *The Pioneers.*

co-op'er-ate, 1 ko-ŏp'ər-ēt; 2 eo-ŏp'-er-āt, *vi.* [*co-op'er-at″ed; co-op'er-at″ing.*] To work together for a common object. —**co-op″er-a'tion,** *n.*

co-op'er-a-tive, 1 ko-ŏp'ər-ə-tiv; 2 eo-ŏp'er-a-tĭv, *a.* **1.** Working or willing to

---

1: ɑrtistic, ārt; fat, fāre; fast; get, prēy; hit, polīce; obey, gō; net, ēr; full, rūle; but, būrn;
2: ärt, āpe, făt, fâre, fȧst, sofa; mē, gĕt, prẹy, fẽrn, over; hĭt, īce; ĭ = ē; ı̄ = ẽ; gō, nŏt, ôr, wȯn,

work towards a common good; as, *coopera-tive* pupils. **2.** Working together in a busi-ness where profits and losses are shared; as, a *cooperative* cafeteria. —**co-op′er-a-tive-ly,** *adv.* —**co-op′er-a-tive-ness,** *n.*

co-or′di-nate, 1 ko-ôr′di-nēt; 2 ɛo-ôr′di-nāt, *vt.* & *vi.* [*co-or′di-nat″ed; co-or′di-nat″ing.*] To put or be in the same rank, class, or order, or in harmonious working relation; as, the principal *coordinates* the work of the teachers.

co-or′di-nate, 1 ko-ôr′di-nɪt; 2 ɛo-ôr′di-nat. *a.* Of the same order or rank; exist-ing together in similar relation; as, *coordi-nate* terms. —**co-or′di-nate,** *n.* —**co-or′di-nate-ly,** *a.* —**co-or″di-na′tion.** *n.*

coot, 1 küt; 2 ɛoot, *n.* **1.** A web-footed water bird of the rail family, living near lakes or pools. **2.** A scoter, or surf duck.

cope, 1 kōp; 2 ɛōp, *vi.* [*coped; cop′ing.*] To contend on equal terms; oppose or resist; as, to *cope* with adversity.

Coot (1).

cope, *n.* **1.** Anything that arches over-head; a coping. **2.** A long mantle, especial-ly one worn by priests or bishops.

Co″pen-ha′gen, 1 kō″pn-hē′gn; 2 ɛō″-pn-hā′gn, *n.* Seaport, capital, and largest city of Denmark: officially, **Köbenhavn.**

Co-per′ni-cus, 1 ko-pūr′ni-kus; 2 ɛo-pĕr′ni-ɛŭs, *n.* **Nicholas** (1473-1543), Po-lish astronomer; in 1543 announced dis-covery that the earth revolves on its axis and rotates around the sun.

cop′ing, 1 kōp′ɪŋ; 2 ɛōp′ɪŋ, *n.* The top layer or cap of a wall, usually sloping.

co′pi-ous, 1 kō′pɪ-ʊs; 2 ɛō′pɪ-ŭs, *a.* Abundant; ample; as, *copious* notes. —**co′-pi-ous-ly,** *adv.*

cop′per, 1 kɒp′ər; 2 ɛŏp′er. **I.** *a.* Like or made of copper; as, *copper* color; a *copper* kettle. **II.** *n.* **1.** A reddish metal widely used in art and industry, especially as a conductor of heat and electricity. **2.** An article made from this metal. **3.** [U. S.] A cent. —**cop′per-y,** *a.*

cop′per-as, 1 kɒp′ər-əs; 2 ɛŏp′er-as, *n.* A green substance used in dyeing, ink-making, photography, etc.

cop′per-head″, 1 kɒp′-ər-hed″; 2 ɛŏp′er-hĕd″, *n.* **1.** A poisonous North-American snake, with red-dish-brown blotches on its pale-brown skin. **2.** [**Cop-perhead**] During the War between the States, a Copperhead (1). Northerner who was in sympathy with the Southern cause.

cop′per-plate″, 1 kɒp′ər-plēt; 2 ɛŏp′er-plāt, *n.* **1.** A plate of polished copper on which a writing or design is engraved or etched in reverse. **2.** A picture or design printed from such a plate.

cop′pice, 1 kɒp′ɪs; 2 ɛŏp′iɕ, *n.* A low-growing thicket. **copse**‡.

cop′ra, 1 kɒp′rə; 2 ɛŏp′ra, *n.* The dried pulp of the coconut that yields coconut oil.

copse, 1 kɒps; 2 ɛŏps, *n.* Same as *coppice*.

cop′y, 1 kɒp′ɪ; 2 ɛŏp′y. **I.** *vt.* & *vi.* [*cop′ied; cop′y-ing.*] To make a copy of; reproduce; imitate; as, do not *copy* from other stu-dents. **II.** *n.* [*cop′ies*, pl.] **1.** A reproduction or imitation; duplicate. **2.** A single printed pamphlet, book, or the like, of an edition or issue. **3.** A pattern given for imitation: especially, a written or typewritten manu-script to be reproduced in type. **4.** A speci-men for imitation, given as an exercise in writing. —**cop′y-ist,** *n.* **cop′i-er** ‡.

cop′y-right″, 1 kɒp′ɪ-rait″; 2 ɛŏp′y-rīt″. **I.** *vt.* To secure copyright for (as a book or work of art). **II.** *n.* The sole legal right of authors, artists, etc., to publish and sell their works, for a limited time.

co′quet-ry, 1 kō′ket-rɪ; 2 ɛō′kĕt-ry, *n.* [*co′quet-ries*, pl.] Trifling in love; also, the quality of being coquettish.

co-quette′, 1 ko-ket′; 2 ɛo-kĕt′, *n.* A woman who endeavors to attract admira-tion merely to grat-ify her vanity; flirt. —**co-quet′tish,** *a.* —**co-quet′tish-ly,** *adv.*

cor′a-cle, 1 kɒr′-ə-kl; 2 ɛŏr′a-el, *n.* A small fishing-boat of hide or oil-cloth on a wicker frame.

Coracle.

cor′al, 1 kɒr′əl; 2 ɛŏr′al. **I.** *a.* Consisting of or like coral. **II.** *n.* **1.** A lime-like rocky substance secreted by marine polyps for common support and habitation. Coral life grows outward and upward, leaving its center dead. Coral forms reefs and is-lands, and assumes many shapes known as **branch, brain, fan, cup, mushroom, bud, tree,** etc. **2.** A coral-producing animal. **3.** The color of red-coral.

Coral (II, 1).

cord, 1 kērd; 2 ɛôrd. **I.** *vt.* **1.** To bind or secure with cord; furnish with cords. **2.** To pile fire-wood for measurement or sale by the cord. **3.** To ornament or finish with cord. **II.** *n.* **1.** A string of several strands. **2.** A measure for wood, equal to 128 cubic feet. **3.** Corduroy; also, other kinds of ribbed cloth. **4.** A cord-like structure; as, the spinal *cord*. **5.** Any influence that binds.

cord'age, 1 kôrd'ıj; 2 eôrd'aġ, *n.* Ropes and cords collectively; especially, ropes in the rigging of a ship.

cor'dial, 1 kôr'jəl *or* kôrd'yəl; 2 eôr'jal *or* eôrd'yal. **I.** *a.* **1.** Proceeding from the heart; exhibiting or expressing kindliness; hearty; encouraging. **2.** Reviving the spirits; bracing; stimulating. **II.** *n.* **1.** That which stimulates or exhilarates; especially a medicine used for such purpose. **2.** An aromatic spirituous liquor. — **cor'dial-ly,** *adv.*

cor-dial'i-ty, 1 kər-jal'ı-tı *or* kər″dı-al″ı-tı; 2 eôr-jăl'i-ty *or* eôr″di-al'i-ty, *n.* [*cor-dial'i-ties,* pl.] The quality of being cordial; friendliness.

cor″dil-le′ra, 1 kôr″dil-yā′rə *or* kər-dil′-ər-ə; 2 eôr″dĭl-yâ′ra *or* eôr″dĭl′er-a, *n.* A mountain range.

cor'don, 1 kôr'dən; 2 eôr'don, *n.* **1.** An extended line, as of men, ships, forts, etc.; as, a *cordon* of police. **2.** An ornamental lace, cord, ribbon, or coping.

cor'du-roy, 1 kôr'du-rei *or* kər″du-rei′; 2 eôr'du-rŏy *or* eôr″du-rŏy′. **I.** *a.* **1.** Made of corduroy, as trousers. **2.** Formed from logs laid crosswise; as, a *corduroy* road. **II.** *n.* **1.** A thick and very durable cotton cloth, corded or ribbed. **2.** [**corduroys**] Trousers made of corduroy. **3.** A corduroy road.

cord'=wood″, 1 kôrd'=wud″; 2 eôrd'=wood″, *n.* Fire=wood sold by the cord.

core, 1 kôr; 2 eôr. **I.** *vt.* [*cored; cor'ing.*] To remove the core of; as, to *core* an apple. **II.** *n.* **1.** The central, rather woody, innermost part of certain fruits; as, the *core* of an apple or pear. **2.** The innermost part of any thing; heart. **3.** The main idea or pith of a speech or an article. — **cor'er,** *n.*

Cor-fu', 1 kər-fū'; 2 eôr-fu', *n.* A Greek island in the Ionian Sea; also its fortified seaport capital. Ancient **Corcyra.**

Cor'inth, 1 kər'ınth; 2 eôr'inth, *n.* An ancient fortified city in central Greece, notorious for its luxury and dissipation.

Co-rin'thi-an, 1 ko-rin'thı-ən; 2 eo-rĭn'thi-an. **I.** *a.* **1.** Pertaining to Corinth. **2.** Pertaining to the most ornate of the three Greek orders of architecture, marked by a bell=shaped capital encircled with the acanthus leaf design. **II.** *n.* An inhabitant of Corinth. — **Corinthians.** Either of two epistles addressed by the Apostle Paul to the Christians of Corinth.

cork, 1 kôrk; 2 eôrk. **I.** *vt.* **1.** To stop with a cork, as a bottle. **2.** To silence or check; as, to *cork* up laughter or anger. **II.** *n.* **1.** The light, porous outer bark of a tree (the **cork=oak**): used for stoppers for bottles, for floats, etc. **2.** Anything made of cork or serving as a cork. — **corked,** *a.*

cork'screw″, 1 kôrk'skrū″; 2 eôrk'seru″. **I.** *vt. & vi.* To move or cause to move like a corkscrew; twist; as, he *corkscrewed* his way through the crowd. **II.** *a.* Shaped like a corkscrew; spirally twisted; as, *corkscrew* ringlets. **III.** *n.* A spirally shaped instrument for drawing corks from bottles.

cor'mo-rant, 1 kôr'mo-rənt; 2 eôr'mo-rant, *n.* **1.** A large, dark, fish=eating sea=bird, noted for its ravenous appetite. **2.** Hence, a greedy person.

corn, 1 kôrn; 2 eôrn, *vt.* To preserve in salt or brine; as, to *corn* beef. — **corned,** *a.*

corn[1], *n.* **1.** The edible seed of any of the cereal grasses; grain: in England, wheat; in the U. S., Indian corn or maize. **2.** Any plant that produces corn.

corn[2], *n.* A horny thickening of the skin as a result of pressure or friction, especially on the foot.

corn bread. Bread or plain cake made from Indian corn=meal or maize=flour.

corn'=cob″, *n.* **1.** The hard, woody, central portion of an ear of corn. **2.** A pipe for smoking tobacco, made from corn=cob.

cor'ne-a, 1 kôr'nı-ə; 2 eôr'ne-a, *n.* The transparent part of the outer coat of the eyeball.

cor'ner, 1 kôr'nər; 2 eôr'ner. **I.** *vt.* To drive into a corner or a position of difficulty; embarrass; as, to *corner* a witness. **II.** *a.* Belonging to, at, or for, a corner; as, a *corner* store; a *corner* table. **III.** *n.* **1.** An angle formed by the meeting of two or more lines or surfaces; as, the *corner* of a box, room, etc.; also, the space within the angle. **2.** The intersection of two streets. **3.** A retired or remote spot; a nook. **4.** A position of embarrassment or difficulty, from which it is hard to escape; as, he was in a tight *corner.*

cor'ner=stone″, *n.* **1.** A stone uniting two walls at the corner of a building. **2.** Something fundamental or of primary importance; as, Magna Carta, the *corner=stone* of English liberty.

cor'net, 1 kôr'net; 2 eôr'nĕt, *n.* **1.** A small wind=instrument of the trumpet class. **2.** A cone=shaped paper wrapper used to hold candy, etc. — **cor-net'ist** *or* **cor'net-ist,** *n.* One who plays the cornet. **cor-net'tist** ‡.

corn'field″, 1 kôrn'fīld″; 2 eôrn'fēld″, *n.* A field used for the growing of corn; also, a field of corn.

Cornet (1).

corn'=flow″er, *n.* **1.** The corn=cockle. **2.** A plant common to grain fields, bearing pink or blue flower heads: called also *bachelor's=button,* **bluebonnet,** and *bluebottle.*

cor'nice, 1 kôr'nıs; 2 eôr'niç, *n.* A horizontal molded projection at the top of a building, or round the walls of a room close to the ceiling.

1: artistic, ärt; fat, fâre; fast; get, prēy; hit, polïce; obey, gō; net, ôr; full, rūle; but, bûrn;
2: ärt, āpe, făt, fâre, fàst, sofa; mē, gĕt, prẹy, fẽrn, over; hĭt, īce; ĭ = ē; ĭ = ĕ; gō, nŏt, ôr, wọn,

Cor′nish, 1 kôr′nĭsh; 2 eôr′nĭsh. **I.** *a.* Of or pertaining to Cornwall, its inhabitants, or its language. **II.** *n.* The language formerly spoken in Cornwall.

corn′=starch″, *n.* Starch made from corn or maize, etc., and used for food.

cor″nu-co′pi-a, 1 kôr″niu-kō′pĭ-ə; 2 eôr″nū-eō′pi-a, *n.* [*cor″nu-co′pi-as* or *cor″-nu-co′pi-æ*, pl.] **1.** The horn of plenty, usually shown as overflowing with fruits and flowers, symbolizing plenty **2.** A cone or horn for holding candies.

Corn′wall, 1 kôrn′wōl; 2 eôrn′wạl, *n.* A county in southwestern England.

co-rol′la, 1 ko-rŏl′ə; 2 eo-rŏl′a, *n.* In botany, the inner circle or set of leaves of a flower, composed of petals.

co-ro′na, 1 ko-rō′nə; 2 eo-rō′na, *n.* [*co-ro′nas* or *co-ro′nae*, 1 ko-rō′nĭ; 2 eo-rō′-nē, pl.] **1.** A circle of light around one of the heavenly bodies, as, the sun during a total eclipse. **2.** In botany, a crown-like process at the top of the tube of the corolla. See *milkweed*.

cor″o-na′tion, 1 kŏr″o-nē′shən; 2 eôr″-o-nā′shon, *n.* The act or ceremony of crowning a monarch.

cor′o-ner, 1 kŏr′o-nər; 2 eôr′o-ner, *n.* A public officer who inquires into the cause of sudden or violent death.

cor′o-net, 1 kŏr′o-net; 2 eôr′o-nĕt, *n.* **1.** A small crown worn by a noble of lower rank than a ruler; as, an earl's *coronet*. **2.** Any ornamental wreath or band for the head, especially one worn by women.

Corp. Abbreviation of *Corporal, Corporation.*

cor′po-ral, 1 kôr′po-rəl; 2 eôr′po-ral, *a.* Belonging or relating to the body as opposed to the mind.

cor′po-ral, *n.* The lowest non=commissioned officer in a company of soldiers, the leader of a squad of eight men.

cor′po-rate, 1 kôr′po-rĭt; 2 eôr′po-rat, *a.* **1.** Legally associated for the transaction of business; incorporated. **2.** Belonging to a corporation. — **cor′po-rate-ly**, *adv.*

cor″po-ra′tion, 1 kôr″po-rē′shən; 2 eôr″po-rā′shon, *n.* A body of persons legally associated for the transaction of business and acting as a single person.

cor-po′re-al, 1 kôr-pō′rɪ-əl; 2 eôr-pō′re-al, *a.* Having a body; of a material nature; physical: opposed to *immaterial* or *spiritual.* — **cor-po′re-al-ly**, *adv.*

corps, 1 kōr; 2 eôr, *n.* [*corps*, 1 kōrz; 2 eôrs, pl.] **1.** A number of persons united in some special work; as, a *corps* of street=cleaners. **2.** A large section of an army containing two or more divisions. **3.** A special military department.

corpse, 1 kôrps; 2 eôrps, *n.* A dead body.
 Syn.: carcass, remains.

cor′pu-lent, 1 kôr′piu-lent; 2 eôr′pū-lĕnt, *a.* Having a great excess of fat. — **cor′-pu-lence, cor′pu-len-cy**, *n.* — **cor′pu-lent-ly**, *adv.*

cor′pus-cle, 1 kôr′pus-l; 2 eôr′pŭs-l, *n.* A minute cell found free in the blood or incorporated in bone.

cor-ral′, 1 kə-ral′; 2 eŏ-răl′, **I.** *vt.* [*cor-ralled′; cor-ral′ling.*] [Western U. S.] **1.** To drive into and enclose in a corral; pen up; as, to *corral* horses. **2.** To arrange in the form of a corral; as, to *corral* wagons. **II.** *n.* **1.** An enclosed space or pen for livestock. **2.** A camping=place surrounded by wagons for defense.

cor-rect′, 1 kə-rekt′; 2 eŏ-rĕet′. **I.** *vt.* **1.** To remove faults or errors from; set right; rectify; as, to *correct* a statement. **2.** To make right; amend; remedy; as, to *correct* a mistake. **3.** To chastise; punish; as, to *correct* a child. **II.** *a.* Free from fault or mistake; true, right, or proper; suitable; as, *correct* style or behavior. — **cor-rect′ly**, *adv.* — **cor-rect′ness**, *n.* — **cor-rec′tor**, *n.*

cor-rec′tion, 1 kə-rek′shən; 2 eŏ-rĕe′-shon, *n.* **1.** The act of correcting or setting right; rectification. **2.** That which is offered as an improvement; as, *corrections* on a proof=sheet. **3.** The act or process of disciplining or punishing; as, the wayward boy was sent to a house of *correction*.

cor-rec′tive, 1 kə-rek′tɪv; 2 eŏ-rĕe′tiv. **I.** *a.* Tending to correct or set right; as, the *corrective* diet. **II.** *n.* That which corrects or counteracts anything injurious.

cor″re-late′, 1 kŏr″ɪ-lēt′; 2 eŏr″e-lāt′. *vt.* & *vi.* [*cor″re-lat′ed; cor″re-lat′ing.*] To link together in a systematic way; connect; as, to *correlate* the study of botany and zoology. — **cor″re-la′tion**, *n.*

cor-rel′a-tive, 1 kə-rel′ə-tiv; 2 eŏ-rĕl′a-tĭv. **I.** *a.* Having mutual relationship; as, *correlative* terms. **II.** *n.* **1.** One of two or more persons or things united by reason of some natural relation or correspondence; as, father and son are *correlatives*. **2.** In grammar, either of two terms used together, as "neither" and "nor".

cor″re-spond′, 1 kŏr″ɪ-spɒnd′; 2 eŏr″e-spŏnd′, *vi.* **1.** To be equal or adequate; as, let the severity of punishment *correspond* to the gravity of the crime. **2.** To be mutually suitable; to agree; as, clownishness does not *correspond* with dignity. **3.** To answer or conform to the description of something else; be similar; agree in details; as, the pictures *correspond*. **4.** To communicate by means of letters.

cor″re-spon′dence, 1 kŏr″ɪ-spon′dens; 2 eŏr″e-spŏn′dĕnç, *n.* **1.** The act, condition, or state of corresponding; fitness; agreement; similarity; as, *correspondence* between two statements. **2.** Communication by letters; also, the letters.

1: ə = final; ɪ = habit; aisle; au = out: ɒil; iu = feud; chin; go; ʜ = loch; ŋ = sing; thin, this.
2: wọlf, dọ; bŏŏk, bōōt; fụll, rụle, cūre, bŭt, bûrn; ŏil; e = k; ḡo, ģem; iŋk; ç = s; thin, this.

cor″re-spon′dent, 1 kŏr″ĭ-spon′dent; 2 eŏr″e-spŏn′dĕnt. **I.** *a.* Having correspondence; suitable; fit; adapted. **II.** *n.* One who writes letters to another, as a friend, business associate in another city, or a contributor to a newspaper or magazine.

cor′ri-dor, 1 kŏr′ĭ-dẽr; 2 eŏr′ĭ-dŏr, *n.* A wide gallery; a passageway in a building, usually with rooms opening into it.

cor-rob′o-rate, 1 ke-rŏb′o-rēt; 2 eŏ-rŏb′o-rāt, *vt.* [cor-rob′o-rat″ed; cor-rob′o-rat″ing.] To give additional strength to, as a conviction; confirm; as, the teacher *corroborated* his story. — **cor-rob′o-rat″er,** *n.* — **cor-rob″o-ra′tion,** *n.* — **cor-rob′o-ra-tive,** *a.* **cor-rob′o-ra-to-ry** ‡.

cor-rode′, 1 ke-rōd′; 2 eŏ-rōd′, *v.* [cor-rod′ed; cor-rod′ing.] **I.** *t.* To eat away gradually; rust; as, moisture *corrodes* iron. **II.** *i.* To become rusted; suffer corrosion; waste away; as, the metal *corrodes.*

cor-ro′sion, 1 ke-rō′ʒen; 2 eŏ-rō′zhon, *n.* A gnawing or wearing away; gradual decay; as, the *corrosion* of morality.

cor-ro′sive, 1 ke-rō′sĭv; 2 eŏ-rō′sĭv. **I.** *a.* Having the power of corroding or destroying; as, a *corrosive* acid. **II.** *n.* That which corrodes; a corroding agent, as an acid; or, figuratively, grief, time, etc. — **cor-ro′sive-ly,** *adv.* — **cor-ro′sive-ness,** *n.*

cor′ru-gate, 1 kŏr′u-gēt; 2 eŏr′u-gāt. **I.** *vt.* & *vi.* [cor′ru-gat″ed; cor′ru-gat″ing.] To form into alternate ridges and furrows; wrinkle. **II.** *a.* Formed into alternate ridges and furrows. **cor′ru-gat″ed** ‡. — **cor″ru-ga′tion,** *n.*

cor-rupt′, 1 ke-rupt′; 2 eŏ-rŭpt′. **I.** *vt.* To exert a bad influence upon; spoil; degrade; debase; subject to decay; also, to deprave; pollute; pervert, as by bribery. **II.** *vi.* To become rotten; putrefy; degenerate. **III.** *a.* **1.** Changed to a spoiled state; tainted; putrid. **2.** Of a perverted character; given to bribery; dishonest. — **cor-rupt′er, cor-rupt′or,** *n.* — **cor-rup′tive,** *a.* — **cor-rupt′ly,** *adv.* — **cor-rupt′ness,** *n.*
    SYN.: bad, debauched, immoral.

cor-rupt′i-ble, 1 ke-rupt′ĭ-bl; 2 eŏ-rŭpt′ĭ-bl, *a.* **1.** Subject to decay, as flesh. **2.** Open to bribery; as, the mayor was not *corruptible.* — **cor-rupt″i-bil′i-ty,** *n.*

cor-rup′tion, 1 ke-rup′shen; 2 eŏ-rŭp′shon, *n.* **1.** The act of decaying; rottenness. **2.** The causing of a person to be dishonest; bribery. **3.** Lack of moral principle; loss of purity; dishonesty.

cor′sage, 1 kŏr′sɪj *or* (F.) kŏr″sāʒ′; 2 eŏr′saġ *or* (F.) eŏr″säzh′, *n.* **1.** The waist of a woman's dress. **2.** A bouquet of flowers worn at the waist.

cor′sair, 1 kŏr′sār; 2 eŏr′sâr, *n.* **1.** Formerly, a Turkish or Saracen pirate who plundered Christian ships and attacked the coasts of Christian countries. **2.** A pirate; freebooter; also, his ship.

corse′let, 1 kŏrs′let; 2 eŏrs′lĕt, *n.* In the Middle Ages, the body armor of a knight, especially the breastplate. **cors′let** ‡.

cor′set, 1 kŏr′set; 2 eŏr′sĕt, *n.* A close-fitting laced and stiffened undergarment worn by women about the waist and hips.

Cor′si-ca, 1 kŏr′sɪ-ke; 2 eŏr′si-ea, *n.* A French island in the Mediterranean Sea; 3,367 square miles. — **Cor′si-can,** *a.* & *n.*

Cor′tez, 1 kŏr′tez *or* (Sp.) kor-tĕs′; 2 eŏr′tĕz *or* (Sp.) cōr-tĕs′, *n.* **Hernando** (1485-1547), Spanish military explorer and conqueror of Mexico. **Cor′tes** ‡.

cor′tex, 1 kŏr′-teks; 2 eŏr′tĕks, *n.* [cor′ti-ces, 1 kŏr′tĭ-sīz; 2 eŏr′ti-cĕs, pl.] **1.** The bark or rind of a tree or fruit. **2.** The outer layer of the brain. — **cor′ti-cal,** *a.*

cor′ti-sone, 1 kŏr′tɪ-sōn; 2 eŏr′ti-sōn, *n.* A powerful substance extracted from the adrenal glands and sometimes used in the treatment of rheumatic disorders.

cos-met′ic, 1 kez-met′ɪk; 2 eŏs-mĕt′ie. **I.** *a.* Pertaining to the beautifying of the complexion; as, a *cosmetic* cream. **II.** *n.* Anything made to improve the appearance of the skin and hair, as creams, powders, lipsticks, rinses, etc.

cos′mic, 1 kez′mɪk; 2 eŏs′mie, *a.* Pertaining to the universe or cosmos; hence, orderly; vast. — **cos′mic rays.** Any of the extremely penetrating rays which seem to come from beyond the earth's atmosphere.

cos″mo-pol′i-tan, 1 kez″mo-pel′i-ten; 2 eŏs″mo-pŏl′i-tan. **I.** *a.* **1.** Common to all the world; not local or limited; as, a *cosmopolitan* outlook. **2.** At home in all parts of the world; unprejudiced; having wide interests; as, a *cosmopolitan* traveller. **II.** *n.* A citizen of the world; a person of wide interests and no prejudices.

cos′mos, 1 kez′mos; 2 eŏs′mŏs, *n.* **1.** The world or universe as a system perfect in order or arrangement: opposed to *chaos.* **2.** Hence, any harmonious system; order. **3.** A plant of the aster family, with white, pink, or rose-colored flowers which bloom in the fall.

Cosmos (3).

Cos′sack, 1 kes′ak; 2 eŏs′ăk, *n.* A member of a people in southern Russia, famed for horsemanship and formerly largely comprising the cavalry of the armies of the czars.

cost, 1 kest *or* kēst; 2 eŏst *or* eŏst. **I.** *vt.* & *vi.* [cost; cost′ing.] **1.** To be had for a price; as, the book *costs* a dollar. **2.** To cause the loss of; as, the battle *cost* hundreds of lives.

3. To cause payment or loss. **II.** *n.* **1.** The price paid for anything; outlay; charge; as, the *cost* of an automobile. **2.** The labor, loss, or suffering involved in anything.

Cos′ta Ri′ca, 1 kəs′tə rī′kə; 2 cŏs′ta rī′ca. A republic of Central America; area, about 23,000 square miles.

cos′ter-mon″ger, 1 kəs′tər-muŋ″gər; 2 cŏs′ter-mŏn″ger', *n.* One who sells fruits, vegetables, etc., on the streets.

cos′tive, 1 kəs′tɪv; 2 cŏs′tiv, *a.* Constipated. —**cos′tive-ly,** *adv.* —**cos′tive-ness,** *n.*

cost′ly, 1 kəst′lɪ; 2 cŏst′ly, *a.* [*cost′li-er; cost′li-est.*] Of great cost; expensive; as, *costly* furs. —**cost′li-ness,** *n.*

SYN.: dear, precious, sumptuous, valuable.

cos-tume′ 1 kəs-tiūm′; 2 cŏs-tūm′, *vt.* To furnish with costumes, as a person; equip, as a play. —**cos-tum′er,** *n.*

cos′tume, 1 kəs′tiūm; 2 cŏs′tūm, *n.* The garments, collectively, worn at one time; dress, especially of a country, period, class, etc.; as, a hunting *costume.*

co′sy, 1 kō′zɪ; 2 cō′zy, *a.* Same as *cozy.*

cot[1], 1 kət; 2 cŏt, *n.* A cottage.

cot[2], *n.* A light, portable bedstead.

cote, 1 kōt; 2 cōt, *n.* A sheep=fold, or a place of shelter; as, a dove=*cote.*

co″te-rie′, 1 kō″tə-rī′ *or* kō′tə-rī; 2 cō″-te-rē′ *or* cō′te-rē, *n.* A group or set of persons who meet habitually; a clique.

co-til′lion, 1 ko-til′yən; 2 co-tĭl′yon, *n.* **1.** A square dance; quadrille. **2.** The music for such a dance.

cot′tage, 1 kət′ɪj; 2 cŏt′aġ, *n.* **1.** A humble dwelling; small house. **2.** [U. S.] An out=of=town residence, often a large mansion at a summer resort. —**cot′tag-er,** *n.*

cot′ter[1], 1 kət′ər; 2 cŏt′er, *n.* In Scotland, the holder of a small farm. **cot′tar** ‡.

cot′ter[2], *n.* A metal pin or key, used to fasten together two parts of machinery, as a wheel on its shaft. **cotter=pin** ‡.

Cotton (1).

a, the boll ready for picking.

cot′ton, 1 kot′n; 2 cŏt′n, *n.* **1.** The soft fibrous material enclosing the seeds of the cotton=plant. **2.** The plant which bears this down. **3.** Cotton cloth or thread. —**cot′ton,** *a.* —**cot′ton-y,** *a.* Resembling cotton.

cot′ton-mouth″, 1 kət′n-mauth″; 2 cŏt′n-mouth″, *n.* [Southern U. S.] A poisonous snake, the water=moccasin.

cot′ton-seed″, 1 kət′n-sīd; 2 cŏt′n-sēd,

n. The seed of the cotton=plant. —**cot′ton-seed=meal″,** *n.* Cottonseed, ground after removing the oil: used in feeding cattle, and as a fertilizer. —**cot′ton-seed=oil″,** *n.* The oil obtained from cottonseed.

cot′ton-tail″, 1 kət′n-tēl″; 2 cŏt′n-tāl″, *n.* The common American gray rabbit.

cot′ton-wood″, 1 kət′n-wud″; 2 cŏt′n-wŏŏd″, *n.* **1.** Any American variety of poplar tree, having seeds covered with a white, cottony down. **2.** The wood of this tree.

cot″y-le′don, 1 kət″ɪ-lī′dən; 2 cŏt″y-lē′don, *n.* A seed=leaf, or the first leaf which pushes out from a seed.

couch, 1 kauch; 2 couch. **I.** *vt.* **1.** To cause to lie or recline, as on a bed. **2.** To lower for attack; as, to *couch* a lance. **3.** To express, imply, or conceal in words; as, to *couch* a request tactfully. **II.** *vi.* To lie down; rest; crouch; hide; lurk; as, the lion *couched* in the brush. **III.** *n.* A bed or other support for sleeping or reclining.

cou′gar, 1 kū′gər; 2 cu′gar, *n.* A large animal of the cat family, tawny in color, found throughout the American continents; also called **catamount, puma, panther, mountain=lion.**

cough, 1 kɔf; 2 côf. **I.** *vt.* **1.** To expel from the breathing=tubes by a cough; as, to *cough* up phlegm. **2.** To produce (some result) by coughing; as, he *coughed* himself red in the face. **II.** *vi.* To expel air from the lungs in a spasmodic, noisy manner; as, he *coughed* continually. **III.** *n.* **1.** A sudden, harsh expulsion of breath. **2.** A disease marked by coughing.

could, 1 kud; 2 cud. [Past tense of *can.*] **1.** Had the knowledge or ability to; as, he *could* read; he *could* swim. **2.** Should or would be able to; as, you *could* get well, if you would take your medicine. **3.** Be allowed to; as, he *could* go and play, if his lessons were done. **4.** Had a right to; as, ancient kings *could* judge their subjects. **5.** To feel like doing; as, I *could* shout for joy.

cou′lee, 1 kū′li; 2 cu′lĭ, *n.* In western North America, a deep gulch, usually dry, with sloping slides. Also, **cou′lée,** 1 kū′lē; 2 cu′le.

coun′cil, 1 kaun′sɪl; 2 coun′çil, *n.* **1.** A group of persons called together to consult, deliberate, or give advice; as, a *council* of physicians. **2.** A group elected or appointed to make or administer laws.

coun′cil-man, 1 kaun′sɪl-man; 2 coun′-çil-măn, *n.* [*coun′cil-men,* pl.] A member of a town or city council.

coun′cil-or, 1 kaun′sɪl-ər *or* -ər; 2 coun′-çil-or, *n.* A member of a governing body; as, a governor's *council.* **coun′cil-lor** ‡.

coun′sel, 1 kaun′sel; 2 coun′sĕl. **I.** *vt.* [*coun′seled* or *coun′selled; coun′sel-ing* or *coun′sel-ling.*] **1.** To advise; as, I *counsel* you to run. **2.** To urge or recommend; as, to *counsel* silence. **II.** *vi.* To consult; deliberate; as, they *counseled* together. **III.** *n.* **1.** Mutual interchange of opinion; consultation; as, we took *counsel* together. **2.** Opinion; advice; as, to give *counsel*. **3.** Good judgment; prudence; caution; as, in this undertaking, use *counsel*. **4.** A lawyer hired to give advice or to act as an advocate in court. —**coun′sel-or**, *n.* **coun′sel-lor** †. —**counselor at law**, a lawyer.

count, 1 kaunt; 2 count. **I.** *vt.* **1.** To call off the units of, one by one, in order to find out the total number; add; compute; as, to *count* one's money. **2.** To say the numerals in order; as, *count* five. **3.** To believe to be; judge; think; as, to *count* all women wise. **4.** To include in a reckoning; as, *count* every other one. **II.** *vi.* **1.** To call off numbers in order. **2.** To carry weight; matter; as, every vote *counts*. **3.** To rely; depend; as, we *count* on your help. **III.** *n.*[1] **1.** The act of counting; number. **2.** The number counted.—**count′a-ble.** *a.*

count[2], *n.* In France, Spain, Italy, etc., a nobleman originally of the same rank as an earl in England.

count′down, 1 kaunt′daun; 2 count′down, *n.* A time interval measured in a descending order of units to the zero point at which some event is to take place.

coun′te-nance, 1 kaun′tɪ-nəns; 2 coun′te-nanç. **I.** *vt.* [*coun′te-nanced; coun′te-nanc-ing.*] To approve; encourage; as, to *countenance* theft. **II.** *n.* **1.** One's face or features, especially as indicating disposition or state of mind; as, a pleasant *countenance*. **2.** Approval; support; as, he gave no *countenance* to the scheme. **3.** Poise, mental composure.

coun′ter, 1 kaun′tər; 2 coun′ter, *v.* **I.** *t.* **1.** To return, as a blow, by another blow. **2.** To oppose; contradict. **II.** *i.* To make a contrary move, as in fighting.

count′er[1], *n.* **1.** One who or that which counts; especially, a machine for counting. **2.** A piece of wood, ivory, etc., used in counting or scoring. **3.** A table on which to count money or expose goods for sale.

coun′ter[2], *n.* **1.** An opposite, or that which is opposite. **2.** In boxing, a parry; counter=blow. **3.** The part of a shoe that surrounds the heel of the wearer.

coun′ter, *adv.* Contrary; reversely; as, he ran *counter* to our wishes.

coun″ter-act′, 1 kaun″tər-akt′; 2 coun″ter-äet′, *vt.* To act in opposition to.

coun″ter-bal′ance, 1 kaun″tər-bal′əns; 2 coun″ter-băl′anç, *vt.* [*coun″ter-bal′anced; coun″ter-bal′anc-ing.*] To oppose with an equal force; weigh against with an equal weight; offset.

coun′ter-bal″ance, 1 kaun′tər-bal″-

əns; 2 coun′ter-băl″anç, *n.* **1.** Any power or influence equally offsetting another. **2.** Specifically, a weight that balances another.

coun′ter-claim″, 1 kaun′tər-klēm″; 2 coun′ter-claim″, *n.* A claim declared by a defendant in his favor against the plaintiff.

coun′ter-feit, 1 kaun′tər-fit; 2 coun′ter-fĭt. **I.** *vt.* To make something unlawfully, as money; imitate, with intent to deceive; hence, to feign; pretend; as, to *counterfeit* sickness. **II.** *a.* Resembling or made to resemble some genuine thing, with intent to defraud; imitated; as, a *counterfeit* dollar. **III.** *n.* Something, as a coin, made fraudulently to resemble the genuine.—**coun′-ter-feit″er,** *n.* —**coun′ter-feit″ing,** *n.*

coun″ter-mand′, 1 kaun″tər-mand′; 2 coun″ter-månd′, *vt.* **1.** To recall or revoke, as an order. **2.** To contradict or cancel.

coun″ter-march′, 1 kaun″tər-märch′; 2 coun″ter-märch′, *vt.* To march back. — **coun′ter-march″,** *n.* A change of front.

coun′ter-pane″, 1 kaun′tər-pēn″; 2 coun′ter-pān″, *n.* A coverlet for a bed.

coun′ter-part″, 1 kaun′tər-pärt″; 2 coun′ter-pärt″, *n.* **1.** A person or thing precisely like another; a facsimile. **2.** Something corresponding reversely, as the right hand to the left; an opposite.

coun′ter-point″, 1 kaun′tər-point″; 2 coun′ter-pŏint″, *n.* In music, the art of adding to a melody a part or parts that shall harmonize with it, and at the same time be melodious; also, the parts so added.

coun″ter-poise′, 1 kaun″tər-poiz′; 2 coun″ter-pŏiş′, *vt.* [*coun″ter-poised′; coun″-ter-pois′ing.*] To bring to a balance or poise by opposing with an equal weight; counterbalance. —**coun′ter-poise″,** *n.*

coun′ter=rev″o-lu′tion, *n.* A revolution for the purpose of opposing another. —**coun′ter=rev″o-lu′tion-a″ry,** *a. & n.*

coun′ter-sign″, 1 kaun′tər-sain″; 2 coun′ter-sīn″. **I.** *vt.* To sign alongside of or in addition to the signature of another. **II.** *n.* **1.** A secret word or phrase to be given, as to a sentry; a watch=word. **2.** A counter=signature.

coun″ter-sink′, 1 kaun″tər-siŋk′; 2 coun″ter-sĭnk′, *vt.* [*coun″ter-sunk′; coun″-ter-sink′ing.*] **1.** To cut or shape a hollow place, as for the head of a screw. **2.** To sink, as a bolt or screw, into a hollowed=out place. —**coun′ter-sink″,** *n.*

count′ess, 1 kaunt′es; 2 count′ĕs, *n.* The wife of a count, or, in Great Britain, of an earl; also, any woman who possesses an earldom in her own right.

count′ing=house″, *n.* An office for carrying on the business and keeping the accounts of a commercial or other establishment. **count′ing=room″** ‡.

1: αrtistic, ārt; fat, fāre; fast; get, prēy; hit, police; obey, gō; net, ôr; full, rūle; but, būrn;
2: ärt, āpe, făt, fâre, fȧst, sofa; mē, gĕt, prẹy, fẽrn, over; hĭt, īce; ɪ̈=ē; ɪ=ẽ; gō, nŏt, ôr, wȯn,

count′less, 1 kaunt′les; 2 eount′lĕs, *a.* That can not be counted; innumerable.

coun′try, 1 kŭn′trı; 2 eŭn′try. *n.* [*coun′tries,* pl.] **1.** A land under a certain government; a nation. **2.** The land of one's birth or allegiance. **3.** A tract of land; a region; as, a hilly *country.* **4.** A rural or farming district, as opposed to the city; as, a summer in the *country.* **5.** The general public; as, the *country* hated him. — **coun′try,** *a.* — **coun′try-man,** *n.* [*coun′try-men,* pl.] **1.** One living in the country; a rustic. **2.** An inhabitant of a particular country or one of the same country as another; a compatriot. — **coun′try-wom″an,** *n. fem.* — **coun′try=seat″,** *n.* A dwelling or mansion in the country. — **coun′try-side″,** *n.* A section of a country, or its inhabitants.

coun′ty, 1 kaun′tı; 2 eoun′ty, *n.* [*coun′ties,* pl.] **1.** A civil division of a state or kingdom. **2.** The inhabitants of a county; as, the *county* likes its new sheriff.

coup, 1 kū; 2 eu, *n.* A sudden telling blow; a master=stroke.

cou″pé′, 1 kū″pē′; 2 eu″pe′, *n.* **1.** A low four = wheeled two= seated closed carriage. **2.** A closed motor=car with two doors and seats for two to four or five persons.

Coupé (1).

coup′le, 1 kup′l; 2 eŭp′l. **I.** *vt. & vi.* **1.** To join, as one thing to another; connect; unite; as, to *couple* a tractor to a plow. **2.** To join in marriage. **II.** *n.* **1.** Two of a kind; a pair. **2.** Two persons of opposite sex, wedded or otherwise paired; as, many *couples* were dancing. — **coup′ler,** *n.*

coup′let, 1 kup′let; 2 eŭp′lĕt, *n.* Two successive lines of verse, riming together.

coup′ling, 1 kup′lıŋ; 2 eŭp′ling, *n.* **1.** The act of joining together. **2.** A coupler, or that which couples; as, a carriage=*coupling.*

cou′pon, 1 kū′pɒn; 2 eu′pŏn, *n.* A removable portion of a bond, ticket, or the like, certifying that the holder is entitled to some privilege.

cour′age, 1 kur′ıj; 2 eŭr′aġ, *n.* Calmness and fearlessness in the face of danger.
SYN.: boldness, daring, gallantry, valor.

cou-ra′geous, 1 ku-rē′jus; 2 eŭ-rā′ġŭs, *a.* Having or characterized by courage; brave; as, a *courageous* soldier. — **cou-ra′geous-ly,** *adv.* — **cou-ra′geous-ness,** *n.*

cou′ri-er, 1 kū′rı-ər; 2 eu′rier, *n.* A messenger; also, a traveling=attendant.

course, 1 kērs; 2 eôrs. **I.** *vt. & vi.* [*coursed; cours′ing.*] To run or cause to run; run through or over; to hunt (hares) with greyhounds. **II.** *n.* **1.** The act of moving onward; a career; as, our life's *course.* **2.** The way passed over, or the direction taken; as,

a *course* up=hill. **3.** A series of connected motions, acts, or events; as, history's *course.* **4.** Procedure; line of behavior; career; as, the *course* of events; to follow an evil *course.* **5.** The portion of a meal served at one time. **6.** In building, one continuous layer of stone or bricks. **7.** The ground traveled over in certain sports; as, a golf *course.* **8.** A series, as of lectures or lessons.

cours′er, 1 kērs′ər; 2 eôrs′er, *n.* A speedy and spirited horse.

court, 1 kōrt; 2 eôrt, **I.** *vt.* **1.** To make love to; woo; as, to *court* a girl. **2.** To seek the favor of; seek as a favor; solicit; as, to *court* help. **II.** *a.* Of or pertaining to a court; as, *court* customs. **III.** *n.* **1.** A place of justice; also, the presiding judge or judges. **2.** The residence, or the council and following, of a sovereign. **3.** A level place laid out for the playing of a game; as, a tennis or hand=ball *court.* **4.** A space or yard surrounded by walls. **5.** A short street or blind alley. **6.** Servile or flattering attention; as, to pay *court* to a queen.

cour′te-ous, 1 kūr′tı-us; 2 eûr′te-ŭs, *a.* Showing courtesy; polite. — **cour′te-ous-ly,** *adv.* — **cour′te-ous-ness,** *n.*

cour′te-sy, 1 kūr′tı-sı; 2 eûr′te-sy, *n.* [*cour′te-sies,* pl.] **1.** Politeness; also, an act or expression of politeness, kindness, or respect. **2.** Favor or permission; as, to hold a title by *courtesy.* **3.** A curtsy.

court′=house″, *n.* A public building in which judicial courts hold trial.

court′ier, 1 kōrt′yər *or* kōrt′ı-ər; 2 eôrt′-yer *or* eôrt′i-er, *n.* **1.** A member of the royal court circle. **2.** One who seeks favor by flattery and politeness.

court′ly, 1 kōrt′lı; 2 eôrt′ly, *a.* **1.** Pertaining to or befitting a court. **2.** Elegant in manners. — **court′li-ness,** *n.*

court″=mar′tial, *vt.* [*court″=mar′tialed; court″=mar′tial-ing.*] To try, as a soldier or sailor, by court martial. — **court martial.** [*courts mar′tial,* pl.] A court of military or naval officers gathered to try offenses against military or naval law.

court′ship, 1 kōrt′ship; 2 eôrt′shĭp, *n.* The act or period of courting or wooing.

court′yard″, 1 kōrt′yärd″; 2 eôrt′yärd″, *n.* An enclosed yard next to a building, or surrounded by buildings; a court.

cous′in, 1 kuz′n; 2 eŭş′n, *n.* The child of one's uncle or aunt. — **cousin german,** a first cousin. — **cous′in-ly,** *a. & adv.*

cove, 1 kōv; 2 eōv, *n.* **1.** A small bay or sheltered inlet on a coast. **2.** A hollow, or a sheltered valley.

cov′e-nant, 1 kuv′ı-nənt; 2 eov′e-nant. **I.** *vt. & vi.* To enter into a promise by covenant; bind oneself by covenant. **II.**

n. An agreement entered into by two or more persons or parties; a compact; as, an international *covenant.* −cov′e-nant-er, *n.* cov′e-nant-or ‡.

Cov·en-try, 1 kɒv′en-trɪ; 2 ĕŏv′ĕn-try, *n.* A manufacturing town in the midlands of England. −**to send to Coventry,** to banish from society; ostracize.

cov′er, 1 kuv′ər; 2 ĕŏv′er. **I.** *vt.* **1.** To overspread or overlay with something so as to protect or hide; enclose; as, to *cover* the body with a blanket. **2.** To hide or keep from view; cloak; screen; as, weeds *cover* the path. **3.** To meet the extent or requirements of; include; as, this money *covers* all expenses. **4.** To bring under aim and keep in range; as, to *cover* a burglar with a revolver. **5.** To accomplish; pass over; as, he *covered* the distance. **6.** To deal with completely; as, this book *covers* English history. **II.** *n.* **1.** That which is spread or fitted over anything; as, a table=*cover;* also, a lid. **2.** A veil or disguise; pretext. **3.** A shelter or defense; protection. **4.** A thicket or underbrush sheltering game.

cov′er-ing, 1 kuv′ər-ɪŋ; 2 ĕŏv′er-ing, *n.* Anything that covers.

cov′er-let, 1 kuv′ər-let; 2 ĕŏv′er-lĕt, *n.* The outer covering of a bed; a quilt.

cov′ert, 1 kuv′ərt; 2 ĕŏv′ert. **I.** *a.* Concealed; sheltered; secret. **II.** *n.* A shady place or thicket which shelters or conceals, as game. −**cov′ert-ly,** *adv.*

cov′et, 1 kuv′et; 2 ĕŏv′ĕt, *vt.* To desire greatly, especially something that belongs to another.

cov′et-ous, 1 kuv′et-us; 2 ĕŏv′ĕt-ŭs, *a.* Extremely eager to acquire and possess something; as, a *covetous* spirit. −cov′et-ous-ly, *adv.* −cov′et-ous-ness, *n.*

cov′ey, 1 kuv′ɪ; 2 ĕŏv′y, *n.* A flock, as of quails or partridges.

cow, 1 kau; 2 ĕow, *vt.* To make afraid; frighten; daunt; as, to *cow* a person into submission.

cow, *n.* The female of domestic cattle, and of some other animals, such as the seal, elephant, etc.

cow′ard, 1 kau′ərd; 2 ĕow′ard, *n.* One lacking in courage; a craven. −cow′ard-ly, *a.* & *adv.* − cow′ard-li-ness, *n.*

cow′ard-ice, 1 kau′ərd-is; 2 ĕow′ard-ĭç, *n.* The absence of courage; timidity.

cow′bird″, 1 kau′bûrd″; 2 ĕow′bird″, *n.* An American blackbird which builds no nest, but lays its eggs in the nests of other birds. It is often found near cattle. **cow′=black″bird**‡.

Cowbird.

cow′boy″, 1 kau′bɔɪ″; 2 ĕow′bŏy″, *n.* A boy, or, in the western United States, a mounted man, hired to tend cattle.

cow′catch″er, 1 kau′kaĉh″ər; 2 ĕow′-eăch″er, *n.* An iron frame on the front of a locomotive to clear obstacles from the track.

cow′er, 1 kau′ər; 2 ĕow′er, *vi.* To crouch tremblingly; tremble, as, from fear.

cow′herd″, 1 kau′hûrd″; 2 ĕow′hĕrd″, *n.* A person who has care and charge over cattle; a herdsman.

cow′hide″, 1 kau′haid″; 2 ĕow′hīd″. **I.** *vt.* [cow′hid″ed; cow′hid″ing.] To whip with, or as with, a cowhide. **II.** *n.* **1.** The skin of a cow, either before or after tanning. **2.** A whip made of twisted leather.

cowl, 1 kaul; 2 ĕowl, *n.* **1.** A monk's hood; a hooded garment. **2.** A hood=shaped top, as for a chimney. −**cowled,** *a.*

cow′punch″er, 1 kau′punĉh″ər; 2 ĕow′-pŭnch″er, *n.* [U. S.] A cowboy.

cow′ry, 1 kou′rī; 2 ĕow′rē, *n.* A small glossy seashell, some varieties of which are used as money in Africa and others for ornament.

cow′slip″, 1 kau′slɪp″; 2 ĕow′slĭp″, *n.* **1.** An English wild flower of the primrose family; also, an allied or similar American wild flower. **2.** The marsh=marigold.

Cowslip.

cox′comb″, 1 kɒks′-kōm″; 2 ĕŏks′eōm″, *n.* **1.** A conceited, foolish person. **2.** Same as *cockscomb.* **3.** A piece of red cloth notched like a cock's comb, formerly worn in a jester's cap; also, the cap.

cox′swain, 1 kɒk′swēn *or* kŏk′sn; 2 ĕŏk′-swān *or* ĕŏk′sn, *n.* A person who has charge of a rowboat, or launch. **cock′swain** ‡.

coy, 1 kɔɪ; 2 ĕŏy, *a.* **1.** Shrinking from notice or familiar advances; shy. **2.** Pretending to be bashful; coquettish. −coy′-ly, *adv.* −coy′ness, *n.*

co-yo′te, 1 kai-yō′tɪ *or* kai′ōt; 2 ĕī-yō′te *or* ĕī′ōt, *n.* A wild dog=like animal, the prairie=wolf of the western United States and Canada.

coz′en, 1 kuz′n; 2 ĕŏz′n, *vt. & vi.* To cheat in a petty way. − coz′en-age, *n.* − coz′en-er, *n.*

Coyote.

co'zy, 1 kō'zɪ; 2 eō'zy, a. [co'zi-er; co'zi-est.] Snugly and easily comfortable; as, a cozy armchair; contented; sociable. — **co'zi-ly**, adv. — **co'zi-ness**, n.

co'zy, n. [co'zies, pl.] 1. A padded cap or cover for a teapot, to prevent the heat from escaping. 2. A seat in a corner. **co'sy** ‡.

c.p. Abbreviation of candle=power, chemically pure. — **cp.** Abbreviation of compare.— **C.P.A.** Abbreviation of Certified Public Accountant. — **Cr**, abbreviation of chromium. — **cr.** Abbreviation of credit, creditor, crown.

crab, 1 krab; 2 erăb, vi. [crabbed; crabbing. **I.** t. In common speech, to find fault with; decry. **II.** i. To be ill=tempered; as, he crabbed all day.

crab[1], n. 1. A 10=footed creature having the abdomen or tail folded under the body. 2. [Crab] A constellation, Cancer.—**to catch a crab.** In rowing, to sink an oar=blade too deeply; also, to miss the water entirely when making a stroke.

Crab (1).

crab[2], n. Same as crab=apple.

crab[3], n. An ill=tempered, querulous, or surly person. — **crab'bed**, a. — **crab'bed-ly**, adv. — **crab'bed-ness**, n.

crab'=ap"ple, n. A small, sour apple, used chiefly for making preserves; also, the tree bearing this fruit.

crack, 1 krak; 2 erăk, v. **I.** t. 1. To break without separating into pieces; as, to crack china. 2. To cause to give forth a short, sharp sound; as, to crack a whip. 3. To break open, as an egg. 4. To tell with spirit; as, to crack a jest. **II.** i. 1. To split or break; as, the wall cracked. 2. To make a sharp snapping or breaking sound; crackle; as, the ice cracks loudly. 3. To falter; become harsh; as, her voice cracked. 4. To become deranged; as, his brain cracked.

crack, a. Of superior excellence; first=class; as, a crack swimmer.

crack, n. 1. An incomplete separation of two parts of an object, with or without a noticeable space between; a fissure; split; as, a crack in a wall. 2. A sudden and sharp sound; a report, as of a pistol or rifle. 3. A resounding blow. 4. A mental or physical defect; flaw.

crack'er, 1 krak'ər; 2 erăk'er, n. 1. A person or thing that cracks; a firecracker. 2. A thin, brittle biscuit. 3. A low=class white inhabitant of the southeastern U.S.

crack'le, 1 krak'l; 2 erăk'l. **I.** vt. & vi. [crack'led; crack'ling.] 1. To cause to make a snapping or rustling sound; as, to crackle paper. 2. To cover with a network of cracks, as china. 3. To make a series of short, sharp sounds; as, the fire crackles. **II.** n. 1. The sound of crackling. 2. China or pottery having a crackled appearance.

crack'ling, krak'lɪŋ; 2 erăk'ling, n. 1. The action or process of giving out small sharp sounds in rapid succession. 2. The crisp brown skin of roasted pork.

cra'dle, 1 krē'dl; 2 erā'dl, vt. & vi. [cra'dled; cra'dling.] 1. To put into, rest, or rock in, or as in, a cradle. 2. To soothe; nurse; nurture. 3. To reap with a cradle; as, to cradle wheat. 4. To wash, as gold=bearing gravel, in a mining= cradle.

cra'dle, n. 1. A rocking or swinging bed for an infant. 2. A place of birth; origin; as, a cradle of learning. 3. A scythe with wooden finger attachments for harvesting grain. 4. A frame for supporting a ship. 5. A box on rockers for washing gold=bearing dirt.

Cradle.
1. Miners' Cradle or Rocker.
2. Grain=harvesting Cradle.

craft, 1 kraft; 2 erăft, n. 1. Cunning or skill; deceit; guile. 2. Skill or dexterity in any calling, especially in a manual employment. 3. An occupation or employment; as, the craft of builders. 4. A vessel, or vessels collectively; also, an aircraft, or flying=machines collectively.

SYN.: aptitude, art, business, subtlety.

crafts'man, 1 krafts'mən; 2 erăfts'- man, n. [crafts'men, pl.] A skilled mechanic. — **crafts'man-ship**, n.

craft'y, 1 kraft'ɪ; 2 erăft'y, a. [craft'i-er; craft'i-est.] Skilful in deceiving; cunning. — **craft'i-ly**, adv. — **craft'i-ness**, n.

SYN.: astute, designing, sly, tricky, wily.

crag, 1 krag; 2 erăḡ, n. A rough, steep, or broken rock rising or jutting out prominently. — **crag'gi-ness**, n. — **crag'gy**, a.

cram, 1 kram; 2 erăm, vt. & vi. [crammed, cram'ming.] 1. To press together; pack tightly; crowd; as, to cram a hall. 2. To feed to fulness. 3. To force into the mind; as, to cram the memory.

cramp, 1 kramp; 2 erămp, vt. 1. To restrain or confine the action of; hamper. 2. To deflect, as a wagon-wheel, to one side in making a turn; also, to jam (a wheel) by turning too short.

cramp, n. An involuntary, sudden, painful muscular contraction.

cran′ber″ry, 1 kran′ber″ı; 2 erăn′bĕr″y, *n.* [*cran′ber″ries,* pl.] The bright-red acid berry of a plant growing in marshy land, or the plant itself.

crane, 1 krēn; 2 erān, *vt.* [*craned; cran′ing.*] To stretch out or elongate the neck, as a crane.

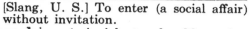

Cranberry.
a, flowering branch; *b,* the fruit, a berry.

crane, *n.* **1.** The largest of the wading birds; all are tall, long-legged, and long-necked, with short, powerful wings, and heron-like appearance. The American species include the **whooping crane,** now rarely seen, the **sand-hill crane,** and the little **brown crane. 2.** In the eastern U. S., the great blue heron. **3.** A hoisting-machine with the added capacity of moving its load in a horizontal direction. **4.** An iron arm used for suspending pots or kettles over a fire.

Crane (1).

cra′ni-um, 1 krē′nı-um; 2 erā′ni-ŭm, *n.* [*cra′ni-a* or *cra′ni-ums,* pl.] **1.** The skull. **2.** That part of the skull enclosing the brain; the brainpan. —**cra′ni-al,** *a.*

crank, 1 kraŋk; 2 erăŋk, *vt. & vi.* To turn a crank, as in starting the engine of an automobile.

crank, *n.* **1.** A bent arm attached to an axis, or a bent portion of an axle, for converting rotary into to-and-fro motion or the reverse. **2.** A bent arm or handle for turning any mechanical device; as, the *crank* of a door-bell or of a motion-picture camera. **3.** A person unreasonably absorbed in a special interest or idea; a fanatic; also, a bad-tempered person.

crank′y, 1 kraŋk′ı; 2 eraŋk′y, *a.* [*crank′-i-er; crank′i-est.*] **1.** Bad tempered; cross. **2.** Liable to upset; easy to tip over, as a canoe. —**crank′i-ly,** *adv.* —**crank′i-ness,** *n.*

cran′ny, 1 kran′ı; 2 erăn′y, *n.* [*cran′nies,* pl.] A narrow opening; a crack.

crape, 1 krēp; 2 erăp, *n.* A thin, gauze-like material. **crêpe**‡.

crash, 1 kraſh; 2 erăsh, *v.* **I.** *t.* **1.** To dash to pieces noisily; shatter. **2.** To force through noisily. **3.** To damage or destroy (an airplane) in landing. **II.** *i.* **1.** To break or fall in pieces with a loud noise; as, the bottles *crashed.* **2.** To drop to the earth, as an airplane out of control. **3.** To collide; as, the automobiles *crashed.* **4.** To collapse suddenly; fail; as, the business *crashed.* **5.**

[Slang, U. S.] To enter (a social affair) without invitation.

crash¹, *n.* **1.** A violent and sudden noise, as of heavy articles falling and breaking; din. **2.** Hence, any similar noise; as, a *crash* of thunder. **3.** Destruction; ruin, especially of a business or of business in general. **4.** A sudden, noisy impact.

crash², *n.* **1.** A course linen fabric used for clothing, toweling, draperies, etc.

crass, 1 kras; 2 erăs, *a.* Dull; stupid. —**crass′ly,** *adv.* —**crass′ness,** *n.*

crate, 1 krēt; 2 erăt. **I.** *vt.* [*crat′ed; crat′-ing.*] To put in a crate. **II.** *n.* A large wickerwork case or framework of slats used for the packing and transporting of articles.

cra′ter, 1 krē′tər; 2 erā′ter, *n.* **1.** The bowl-shaped opening forming the outlet of a volcano. **2.** In military use, the hole caused by the explosion of a mine or shell.

Crater Lake National Park. A park of southwestern Oregon; 249 square miles.

cra-vat′, 1 krə-vat′; 2 era-văt′, *n.* A folded cloth for the neck; a necktie.

crave, 1 krēv; 2 erāv, *vt.* [*craved; crav′ing.*] **1.** To beg for humbly and earnestly; as, to *crave* pardon or mercy. **2.** To long for; desire greatly; as, to *crave* wealth. **3.** To hunger for; as, to *crave* food.

cra′ven, 1 krē′vn; 2 erā′vn. **I.** *a.* Lacking in courage; cowardly; as, a *craven* soldier. **II.** *n.* A base coward. —**cra′ven-ly,** *adv.*

crav′ing, 1 krēv′ıŋ; 2 erāv′ing, *n.* A strong longing or desire.

craw, 1 krɔ; 2 era, *n.* **1.** The first stomach or crop of a bird. **2.** The stomach of any animal.

craw′fish″, 1 krɔ′fiſh″; 2 era′fïsh″, *n.* [*craw′-fish* or *craw′fish″es,* pl.]**1.** A small fresh-water lobster-like shell-fish. **2.** The spiny lobster or sea crawfish.

crawl, 1 krɔl; 2 eral, *vi.* **1.** To move the body slowly along the ground; creep. **2.** To move slowly and feebly; as, a sick person *crawls* about. **3.** To seek influence by servility. **4.** To have a feeling as of crawling things upon the body.

Crawfish (1).

crawl, *n.* **1.** The act of crawling; a creeping motion. **2.** A stroke used in swimming; the crawl-stroke in which the swimmer uses alternate overarm-strokes, and kicks his legs up and down alternately. See illus. on p. 415.—**crawl′er,** *n.*

cray′fish″, 1krē′fiſh″; 2erā′fïsh″,*n.*[*cray′-fish″* or *cray′fish″es,* pl.] A crawfish.

cray′on, 1 krē′ən *or* -en; 2 erā′on *or* -ŏn. **I.** *vt.* To sketch with a crayon. **II.** *n.* **1.** A slender stick of charcoal or colored chalk used for drawing. **2.** A drawing made with crayons.

craze, 1 krēz; 2 erāz. I. *vt. & vi.* [*crazed; craz'ing.*] **1.** To make or become insane. **2.**

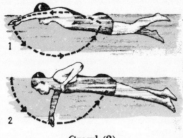

Crawl (2).

1. Left arm entering the water. Dotted line shows direction of stroke back to the hip, and return of the arm to the first position. 2. Right arm in the middle of the stroke and left arm on the return

To make or become full of small cracks or flaws, as pottery. **II.** *n.* **1.** A passing fad or fashion. **2.** Mental disorder. **3.** A flaw in the glaze of pottery. — **crazed,** *a.*

cra'zy, 1 krē'zı; 2 erā'zy, *a.* [*cra'zi-er; cra'zi-est.*] **1.** Unsound in mind; insane; mad. **2.** Shaky; rickety; as, a *crazy* house. **3.** In common speech, extremely fond; foolishly desirous; as, she is *crazy* about dancing. — **cra'zi-ly,** *adv.* — **cra'zi-ness,** *n.*

creak, 1 krīk; 2 erēk. I. *vt. & vi.* To make, or cause to make, a creak. **II.** *n.* A sharp, squeaking sound, as of a rusty hinge.

creak'y, 1 krīk'ı; 2 erēk'y, *a.* [*creak'i-er; creak'i-est.*] Apt to creak; creaking. — **creak'i-ly,** *adv.* — **creak'i-ness,** *n.*

cream, 1 krīm; 2 erēm. I. *vt.* **1.** To skim cream from; hence, to take the best part from. **2.** To add cream to, as tea. **3.** To work butter into a soft, creamlike condition. **4.** To cook with or as with cream; as, to *cream* onions. **II.** *n.* **1.** The rich, yellow, fatty substance which rises to the top of milk; hence, the top or best of anything; as, the *cream* of society. **2.** A delicacy for the table resembling or made of cream; as, ice=cream. **3.** A soft, oily preparation or lotion for the skin.

cream'er-y, 1 krīm'ər-ı; 2 erēm'er-y, *n.* [*cream'er-ies,* pl.] A place for collecting, selling, or keeping cream and butter.

cream'y, 1 krīm'ı; 2 erēm'y, *a.* [*cream'-i-er; cream'i-est.*] Resembling or containing cream. — **cream'i-ness,** *n.*

crease, 1 krīs; 2 erēs, *v.* [*creased; creas'-ing.*] **I.** *t.* To make a crease, fold, or wrinkle in; as, to *crease* paper. **II.** *i.* To become wrinkled. — **creas'er,** *n.*

crease, *n.* The mark of a wrinkle or fold.

cre-ate', 1 krī-ēt'; 2 erē-āt', *vt.* [*cre-at'ed; cre-at'ing.*] To cause to come into existence; cause to be; make, as a work of art.

cre-a'tion, 1 krī-ē'shən; 2 erē-ā'shon, *n.* **1.** The act of creating or forming; as, the *creation* of a new government. **2.** That

which is created; specifically, the universe.

cre-a'tive, 1 krī-ē'tıv; 2 erē-ā'tiv, *a.* Having the power to create; productive.

cre-a'tor, 1 krī-ē'tər; 2 erē-ā'tor, *n.* **1.** One who creates. **2.** [**Creator**] God.

crea'ture, 1 krī'chur *or* -tiur; 2 erē'chur *or* -tūr, *n.* **1.** That which has been created; a living being. **2.** A person dependent upon the power or influence of another.

cre'dence, 1 krī'dens; 2 erē'děnç, *n.* Confidence founded upon external evidence; belief; as, to give *credence* to a report.

cre-den'tials, 1 krī-den'shəlz; 2 erē-děn'shalş, *n. pl.* Papers testifying to the identity, authority, reputation, etc., of some one; references.

cred'i-ble, 1 kred'ı-bl; 2 erěd'i-bl, *a.* Capable of being believed; worthy of confidence or acceptance; as, a *credible* report. — **cred″i-bil'i-ty,** *n.* — **cred'i-bly,** *adv.*

cred'it, 1 kred'ıt; 2 erěd'it. **I.** *vt.* **1.** To accept as true; believe; as, to *credit* a story. **2.** To attribute to or with; as, to *credit* him with courage. **3.** To give credit to or for in an account; as, to *credit* a purchaser with an amount paid. **II.** *n.* **1.** Belief in the truth of a statement or in the sincerity of a person; trust; as, to place *credit* in his story. **2.** A reputation for trustworthiness; character; as, a person of *credit.* **3.** One who or that which adds honor or reputation; as, a student who is a *credit* to his class. **4.** The amount to which a person, corporation, or business house may be financially trusted in a given case. **5.** In an account, the balance in one's favor; as, she has five dollars to her *credit.* **6.** Time allowed for the payment of a debt; as, 20 days' *credit.* — **cred″it-a-bil'i-ty,** *n.* **cred'it-a-ble-ness** ‡.

cred'it-a-ble, 1 kred'ıt-ə-bl; 2 erěd'it-a-bl, *a.* Deserving credit; praiseworthy; meritorious. — **cred'it-a-bly,** *adv.*

cred'i-tor, 1 kred'ıt-ər; 2 erěd'it-or, *n.* One to whom another owes a debt, usually of money.

cre-du'li-ty, 1 krı-diū'lı-tı; 2 ere-dū'li-ty, *n.* A willingness to accept the improbable or the marvelous as true without proof. — **cred'u-lous,** *a.* — **cred'u-lous-ly,** *adv.*

creed, 1 krīd; 2 erēd, *n.* **1.** A formal summary of religious belief; a confession of faith. **2.** That which is believed; doctrine.

creek, 1 krīk; 2 erēk, *n.* **1.** A small inlet, bay, or cove. **2.** [U. S.] An arm of a river; a stream smaller than a river.

creel, 1 krīl; 2 erēl, *n.* **1.** An angler's basket for carrying fish. **2.** A cage of wickerwork for catching lobsters.

creep, 1 krīp; 2 erēp. **I.** *vi.* [*crept; creep'-ing.*] **1.** To move as a serpent; crawl. **2.** To move slowly and secretly; as, the panther *creeps* upon its prey. **3.** To grow along a surface or support, as certain plants. **4.** To have a feeling as of contact with creeping things. **II.** *n.* **1.** The act of creeping. **2.** [**creeps**] A nervous feeling, as of insects creeping on the flesh. —**creep′y,** *a.* —**creep′i-ly,** *adv.* —**creep′i-ness,** *n.*

creep′er, 1 krīp′ər; 2 ɛrēp′er, *n.* **1.** One who or that which creeps. **2.** A creeping or climbing plant. **3.** One of various birds adapted for creeping about trees.

cre-mate′, 1 krī-mēt′ *or* krī′mēt; 2 ɛrē-māt′ *or* ɛrē′māt, *vt.* [*cre-mat′ed; cre-mat′-ing.*] To burn up; reduce to ashes. —**cre-ma′tion,** *n.* —**cre-ma′tor,** *n.*

cre′ma-to-ry, 1 krī′mə-to-rɪ *or* krem′ə-to-rɪ; 2 ɛrē′ma-to-ry *or* ɛrĕm′a-to-ry, *n.* [*cre′ma-to′ries,* pl.] A place for cremating the dead. **cre″ma-to′ri-um** ‡.

Cre′ole, 1 krī′ōl; 2 ɛrē′ōl, *n.* **1.** A native of Spanish America, or of the West Indies, of European parentage. **2.** In Louisiana: (1) A native having French or Spanish ancestors. (2) A native-born Negro. (3) The local French dialect. —**Cre′ole,** *a.*

cre′o-sote, 1 krī′o-sōt; 2 ɛrē′o-sōt, *n.* An oily liquid compound distilled from wood and having a smoky odor and burning taste; it is a powerful antiseptic, and is used to preserve wood and meat.

crêpe, 1 krēp; 2 ɛrep, *n.* See *crape, n.*

cres-cen′do, 1 kre-shen′do *or* kre-sen′do; 2 ɛrĕ-shĕn′do *or* ɛrĕ-sĕn′do. *a. &* *adv.* Slowly increasing in loudness or power of tone. **cres-cen′do,** *n.* An increase in loudness.

cres′cent, 1 kres′ent; 2 ɛrĕs′ĕnt. **I.** *a.* **1.** Increasing: said of the moon in its first quarter. **2.** Crescent-shaped. **II.** *n.* **1.** The visible part of the moon in its first or last quarter; the new or old moon. **2.** Anything shaped like the new moon.

cress, 1 kres; 2 ɛrĕs, *n.* A plant of the mustard family, having a pungent taste and used as a garnish or salad; the watercress.

crest, 1 krest; 2 ɛrĕst. **I.** *vt.* To serve as a crest for; crown; as, clouds *crested* the mountains. **II.** *n.* **1.** A comb or tuft on the head of a fowl. **2.** A projection on the top of a helmet; a plume. **3.** The ridge of a wave or of a mountain; the top of anything. **4.** A heraldic device; coat of arms. **crest′ed,** *a.* —**crest′fall″en,** *a.* Having the crest or head lowered; dispirited; dejected.

Crete, 1 krīt; 2 ɛrēt, *n.* A Greek Island (3,199 square miles) in the eastern Mediterranean. —**Cre′tan,** *a. & n.*

cre-tonne′, 1 krɪ-tən′ *or* krī′tɒn; 2 ɛrē-tŏn′ *or* ɛrē′tŏn, *n.* A strong cotton fabric printed on one side in colored patterns.

Crest (2).

cre-vasse′, 1 krɪ-vas′; 2 ɛre-văs′, *n.* **1.** A deep opening, as in a glacier. **2.** [U. S.] A breach in a levee. —**cre-vassed′,** *a.*

crev′ice, 1 krev′ɪs; 2 ɛrĕv′iç, *n.* A small opening or crack.

crew, 1 krū; 2 ɛrų. An old form of *crowed.*

crew, *n.* **1.** A company of seamen belonging to one ship or boat. **2.** A body of men organized or detailed for a particular work, as to run a train. **3.** A company of people in general; crowd; generally used humorously. **4.** The oarsmen and steersman of a racing boat.

crib, 1 krib; 2 ɛrĭb, *n.* **1.** A rack or manger. **2.** A stall for cattle. **3.** A child's bedstead, with side railings. **4.** A box or bin for grain. **5.** A frame of timber, as to retain a bank of earth. **6.** A translation or unauthorized aid in study.

crib′bage, 1 krib′ɪj; 2 ɛrĭb′aǧ, *n.* A game of cards, played by two to four players.

crick′et[1], 1 krik′et; 2 ɛrĭk′ĕt, *n.* A leaping insect, the male of which makes a chirping sound by friction of the fore wings.

crick′et[2], *n.* An outdoor game played with bats, a ball, and wickets, between two opposing sides numbering eleven each. —**crick′et-er,** *n.* One who plays cricket.

Cricket.

crick′et[3], *n.* A small footstool.

cried, 1 kraɪd; 2 ɛrīd. Past tense and past participle of *cry.*

cri′er, 1 kraɪ′ər; 2 ɛrī′er, *n.* One who announces aloud in public.

cries, 1 kraɪz; 2 ɛrīş. Plural of *cry, n.*; third person singular, present tense, of *cry, v.*

crime, 1 kraɪm; 2 ɛrīm, *n.* **1.** In law, an act that subjects the doer to legal punishment. **2.** Loosely, any evil deed.
SYN.: iniquity, outrage, vice, wrong.

Cri-me′a, 1 kraɪ- *or* krɪ-mī′ə; 2 ɛrī- *or* ɛri-mē′a, *n.* A peninsula on the north coast of the Black Sea. —**Cri-me′an,** *a. & n.*

crim′i-nal, 1 krim′ɪ-nəl; 2 ɛrĭm′i-nal. **I.** *a.* **1.** Relating to crime. **2.** Pertaining to the enforcement of the laws against crime; as, a *criminal* court. **II.** *n.* One who has committed an offense punishable by law. —**crim″i-nal′i-ty,** *n.* —**crim′i-nal-ly,** *adv.*
SYN.: culprit, felon, malefactor, offender.

crimp, 1 krimp; 2 ɛrĭmp. **I.** *vt.* To bend or press into ridges or folds; to wave. **II.** *n.* Anything crimped. —**crimp′er,** *n.*

crim′son, 1 krim′zn; 2 ɛrĭm′şn. **I.** *vt. & vi.* To make or become crimson; redden; blush. **II.** *a.* Of the color called crimson; deep-dyed. **III.** *n.* A red color having a tinge of blue, but lighter than purple.

cringe, 1 krinj; 2 erĭnġ. **I.** *vi.* [*cringed;* *cring'ing.*] **1.** To bow in servility or cowardice; crouch. **2.** To wince; flinch, as in pain. **II.** *n.* A servile crouching. — **crin'ger,** *n.*
SYN.: cower, flinch, quail, quiver, shrink.

crin'kle, 1 kriŋ'kl; 2 erĭn'kl. **I.** *vt. & vi.* [*crin'kled; crin'kling.*] To form or move with folds or wrinkles. **II.** *n.* A wrinkle; a ripple; a twist. — **crin'kly,** *a.*

crin'o-line, 1 krin'o-lin *or* -lĭn; 2 erĭn'o-lĭn *or* -lĭn, *n.* **1.** A stiff elastic fabric; any material for stiffening a skirt, collar, or the like. **2.** A skirt stiffened with such fabric.

crip'ple, 1 krip'l; 2 erĭp'l. **I.** *vt.* [*crip'pled; crip'pling.*] To lame, impair, or disable. **II.** *n.* A person who is lame.

cri'sis, 1 krai'sɪs; 2 erī'sis, *n.* [*cri'ses,* 1 -sĭz; 2 -sēs, pl.] **1.** A turning-point or critical moment in the course of any action. **2.** A sudden or decisive change in the course of a disease, favorable or unfavorable.

crisp, 1 krisp; 2 erĭsp. **I.** *vt. & vi.* To make or become crisp. **II.** *a.* **1.** Well done; firm; brittle; as, *crisp* toast. **2.** Terse or pithy; curt; as, a *crisp* speech. **3.** Fresh; bracing; as, *crisp* air. **4.** Crinkled; lively; as, *crisp* hair. — **crisp'ly,** *adv.* — **crisp'ness,** *n.*

criss'cross", 1 kris'krôs"; 2 erĭs'erôs". **I.** *vt.* To cross with interlacing lines. **II.** *a.* Crossing one another in different directions: said of lines or the like. **III.** *n.* **1.** The cross of one who can not write. **2.** A collection of intersecting lines. **3.** A game played by children. **IV.** *adv.* In different crossing directions; crosswise.

cri-te'ri-on, 1 krai-tī'rɪ-ən; 2 erī-tē'ri-on, *n.* [*cri-te'ri-a or cri-te'ri-ons,* pl.] A standard by which to determine the correctness of a judgment.

crit'ic, 1 krit'ɪk; 2 erĭt'ie, *n.* **1.** One who judges anything by some standard. **2.** One who judges severely. **3.** One who writes professional opinions of art, etc. — **crit'i-cal,** *a.* **1.** Of or pertaining to a critic or criticism. **2.** Disposed or qualified to judge; judicious; fastidious. **3.** Quick to find fault. **4.** Fond of analyzing a thing; exact; thorough. **5.** Of the nature of or preliminary to a crisis; perilous — **crit'i-cal-ly,** *adv.* — **crit'i-cal-ness,** *n.*

crit'i-cize, 1 krit'ɪ-saiz; 2 erĭt'i-çĭz, *v.* [*crit'i-cized; crit'i-ciz"ing.*] **I.** *t.* **1.** To examine critically (a work of literature or art.) **2.** To judge severely; to censure. **II.** *i.* To express critical judgment. **crit'i-cise** ‡. — **crit'i-ciz"a-ble,** *a.* — **crit'i-cism,** *n.*

croak, 1 krōk; 2 erŏk, *v.* **I.** *t.* **1.** To utter by croaking; announce by a croak. **2.** In slang, to kill. **II.** *i.* **1.** To make a harsh guttural sound like that of a frog or raven. **2.** To talk in a doleful tone; forebode evil.

croak, *n.* A hoarse vocal sound as of a frog or raven. — **croak'er,** *n.*

Cro-a'ti-a, 1 kro-ē'shɪ-ə; 2 ero-ā'shi-a, *n.* A republic in Yugoslavia; 21,611 square miles. — **Cro-a'tian,** *a. & n.*

cro-chet', 1 kro-shē'; 2 ero-ehe'. **I.** *vt. & vi.* [*cro-cheted',* 1 kro-shēd'; 2 ero-ehed'; *cro-chet'ing,* 1 kro-shē'ɪŋ; 2 ero-ehe'ing.] To form or knit, as crochet. **II.** *n.* A kind of fancywork produced by looping or entwining thread into a fabric with a hooked needle. — **cro-chet'er,** *n.* — **cro-chet'ing,** *n.*

crock, 1 krok; 2 erŏk, *n.* An earthen pot or jar or other clay vessel.

crock'er-y, 1 krok'ər-ɪ; 2 erŏk'er-y, *n.* Earthenware of any grade, especially kitchen vessels or utensils.

croc'o-dile, 1 krok'o-dail; 2 erŏe'o-dĭl, *n.* A large flesh=eating, air=breathing, lizard=like reptile of America, Africa, and Asia, living largely in warm waters and closely resembling an alligator but having a longer and narrower head. — **crocodile tears,** pretended or false tears; feigned grief.

cro'cus, 1 krō-kus; 2 erō'eŭs, *n.* A small plant of the iris family, with long grass=like leaves and dainty flowers of various hues that blossom in early spring; also, the flower.

Crœ'sus, 1 krī'sus; 2 erē'sŭs, *n.* A wealthy king of Lydia (6th century B.C.); hence, any very wealthy man.

Crom'well, 1 krom'wel *or* krum'wəl; 2 erŏm'wĕl *or* erŏm'wel, *n.* **Oliver** (1599-1658), Lord Protector of England.

crone, 1 krōn; 2 erŏn, *n.* A withered old woman.

cro'ny, 1 krō'nɪ; 2 erō'ny, *n.* [*cro'nies,* pl.] A familiar friend; chum.

crook, 1 kruk; 2 erŏŏk. **I.** *vt. & vi.* To bend; make or grow crooked. **II.** *n.* **1.** A bend or curve; something bent or crooked. **2.** An implement with a crooked or hooked end. **3.** In common speech, a professional criminal; a sharper. — **crook'ed,** *a.* **1.** Not straight; having angles or curves. **2.** Not straightforward; dishonest. — **crook'ed-ly,** *adv.* — **crook'ed-ness,** *n.*
SYN.: awry, bent, deformed, perverse.

croon, 1 krun; 2 erŏŏn, *v.* **I.** *t.* To sing or hum softly, as, she *crooned* a lullaby. **II.** *i.* To make a low, monotonous humming sound; hence, to sing or hum in a deeply sentimental manner. — **croon'er,** *n.*

crop, 1 krop; 2 erŏp, *v.* [*cropped* or *cropt; crop'ping.*] **I.** *t.* **1.** To cut or eat off the stems or the ends of (grasses, vegetables, etc.); also, to gather, as a crop, by plucking or reaping. **2.** To plant for harvest; sow. **3.** To cut off closely, as one's hair or a dog's ears. **II.** *i.* **1.** To appear above the surface: usually with *up* or *out;* as, weeds *crop up* everywhere. **2.** To appear, come, or develop unexpectedly; as, problems *cropped* up. **3.** To eat off the tops of plants and grass: said of sheep, cows, etc.

crop, *n.* **1.** Cultivated plants or grains collectively; also, the soil-product of a particular kind, place, or season; harvest. **2.** The first stomach of a bird; a craw. **3.** A growth of hair or beard, especially when short and stiff. **4.** A hunting- or riding-whip with a leather loop for a lash.

crop'per[1], 1 krɒp'ər; 2 crŏp'er, *n.* **1.** One who raises crops on shares. **2.** A tool for cutting off ends, as of bolts, etc.

crop'per[2], *n.* A heavy, headlong fall, as from a horse. — **to come a cropper,** to fall headlong, as from a horse; hence, to fail disastrously in an undertaking.

cro-quet', 1 kro-kē'; 2 cro-ke', *n.* A lawn-game played by two to eight players with balls, mallets, wire arches, and stakes.

cro-quette', 1 kro-ket'; 2 cro-kĕt', *n.* A ball or cake of previously cooked minced food, fried brown.

cro'sier. See *crozier.*

cross, 1 krɒs; 2 crôs, *vt. & vi.* **1.** To mark, fold, lay, or move across; traverse; intersect. **2.** To cancel, as by crossed lines: with *off* or *out.* **3.** To obstruct; hinder; contradict; irritate. **4.** To make the sign of the cross upon. **5.** To meet and pass; as, her letter *crossed* mine.

cross, *a.* **1.** Resulting from ill-humor; as, a *cross* reply. **2.** Disagreeable; peevish; as, a *cross* teacher. **3.** Transverse; oblique; crossing; as, a *cross* street. **4.** Contrary; entirely different; as, *cross* purposes. — **cross'ly,** *adv.* — **cross'ness,** *n.*

cross, *n.* **1.** An ancient instrument of torture consisting of two crossed timbers, on which a condemned person was fastened and exposed until he died. **2.** [Cross] Christianity, or the Atonement. **3.** Something endured for Christ's sake; trial; tribulation. **4.** A mark or symbol resembling a cross.

cross'=bar", *n.* A transverse bar or line used in any structure. — **cross'=bones",** *n. pl.* A representation of two bones crossing, surmounted by a skull, as a symbol of death. — **cross'bow",** *n.* A weapon having a bow fixed crosswise upon a stock, used during the Middle Ages. — **cross'=bun",** *n.* A circular cake or bun marked with a cross, as eaten on Good Friday. — **cross'=coun"-try,** *a.* Of or pertaining to a route across the country fields and lots.

cross'cut". **I.** *vt. & vi.* [*cross'cut"*; *cross'-cut"ting.*] To cut, saw, or drill transversely or through; run across; intersect. **II.** *a.* **1.** Used or made for the purpose of cutting across the grain of wood; as, a *cross=cut* saw. **2.** Cut on the bias; as, a *cross=cut* silk. **III.** *n.* **1.** A cut across, or a short-cut. **2.** In mining, the level intersecting the lode of the main workings. — **cross'cut"ter,** *n.* — **cross'cut"ting,** *n. & a.*

cross'=ex-am"ine, *vt. & vi.* [*cross'=ex-am"ined; cross'=ex-am"in-ing.*] To question for the purpose of testing the reliability of previous testimony. — **cross'=ex-am"i-na'tion,** *n.* — **cross'=ex-am'in-er,** *n.*

cross'=eyed", *a.* Having one or both eyes focused inward toward the nose. — **cross'=grained',** *a.* **1.** Having the grain gnarled and hard to cut; as, a *cross=grained* board. **2.** Hard to please; cranky.

cross'ing, 1 krɒs'ɪŋ; 2 crôs'ing, *n.* **1.** The place where something, as a waterway, may be crossed; as, a river *crossing.* **2.** An intersection, as of lines or roads. **3.** A passage across a sea, lake, river, etc.; as, the ferry makes two *crossings* a day.

cross'piece", *n.* A piece of material of any kind crossing another. — **cross'=pur"-pose,** *n.* A purpose which opposes another; a conflicting aim; as, to talk at *cross=purposes.* — **cross'=ques"tion,** *vt.* To question minutely; cross-examine. — **cross'=ref"er-ence,** *n.* A reference from one page to another. — **cross'=road",** *n.* A road that crosses another, or that crosses from one main road to another. **cross'=way"**‡. — **cross'roads",** *n.* A place where two or more roads cross. — **cross'=sec"tion,** *n.* **1.** A section cut across anything. **2.** A section of a body at right angles to its length. **3.** A representative number of persons, things, etc., picked from a complete group in order to show the constitution of the whole. — **cross'trees",** *n. pl.* In nautical use, the pieces of wood or iron set crosswise at the head of a mast to extend the shrouds. — **cross'=way",** *n.* A cross-road. — **cross'=ways",** *adv.* Crosswise. — **cross'wise,** *adv.* **1.** Across; as, to set *crosswise.* **2.** In the form of a cross; as, to build a church *crosswise.* **3.** Contrarily; at cross-purposes. — **cross=word puzzle.** See under *puzzle.*

crotch, 1 krɒtʃ; 2 crŏch, *n.* A point of division; fork; as, the *crotch* of a tree; also, a stake or pole with forked top that serves as a support. — **crotched,** *a.*

crotch'et, 1 krɒtʃ'et; 2 crŏch'ĕt, *n.* A whimsical notion; a conceit; an eccentricity. — **crotch'et-i-ness,** *n.* — **crotch'et-y,** *a.*

crouch, 1 krautʃ; 2 crouch, *vi.* **1.** To stoop low, as a person in fear or an animal ready to jump. **2.** To cringe. — **crouch,** *n.*

croup[1], 1 krūp; 2 crup, *n.* A disease of the throat marked by a hard, painful cough and choking. — **croup'y,** *a.*

croup[2], *n.* The rump or portion of a horse's back behind the saddle.

crow, 1 krō; 2 cro, *vi.* [*crowed* or *crew* (old); *crow'ing.*] **1.** To utter the cry of a rooster. **2.** To exalt; boast. **3.** To utter sounds of delight, as an infant.

crow, *n.* **1.** A greedy bird, about 20 inches long, with glossy black plumage. **2.** The rook, or other crow=like bird. **3.** A crow-bar. **4.** The cry of a rooster.

crow′bar″, 1 krō′bär″; 2 erō′bär″, *n.* A straight iron or steel bar, used as a lever.

crowd, 1 kraud; 2 erowd, *v.* **I.** *t.* **1.** To fill to overflowing; pack; as, the people *crowded* the church. **2.** To squeeze closely together; as, they *crowded* us into a small room. **3.** To shove along; push. **4.** In common speech, to press annoyingly; urge; as, he *crowded* me for an answer. **II.** *i.* **1.** To throng together; assemble in multitudes. **2.** To push forward or together.

crowd, *n.* **1.** A numerous collection of persons or things gathered closely together; throng; multitude. **2.** The population in general; mob. **3.** [Slang.] A particular collection of persons; company; gang; clique. SYN.: group, populace, rabble, swarm.

crown, 1 kraun; 2 erown. **I.** *vt.* **1.** To put a crown upon the head of; hence, to invest with royal, imperial, or other high dignity. **2.** To place a wreath or garland upon the head of; hence, to decorate by crowning; as, *crown* him with laurel. **3.** To form the topmost part of; be situated upon the top of; cap; as, a castle *crowns* the hill. **4.** To finish or top off; complete; as, a plum pudding *crowned* the dinner. **5.** To do honor to; as, success *crowned* his labor. **6.** To cause to round upward; make higher at the middle; as, to *crown* a road. **7.** To place a cap or crown upon (a tooth). **8.** In slang, to strike on the head. **II.** *n.* **1.** A decorative circlet or covering for the head, especially as a mark of sovereign power. **2.** A sovereign ruler: with *the;* as, the estate is forfeit to *the crown.* **3.** Sovereignty. **4.** A wreath or garland for the head; as, a *crown* of roses. **5.** A reward; prize. **6.** The top or summit; as, the *crown* of a hill. **7.** The top of the head; as, a bald *crown.* **8.** The upper portion of a hat. **9.** The part of a tooth exposed beyond the gum; especially, the grinding surface of a molar; hence, in dentistry, an artificial substitute for a crown. **10.** A coin; especially, the British five=shilling piece. **11.** The outer point of junction of the two arms of an anchor. —**crown′er**, *n.* —**crown′less**, *a.* —**crown prince**, the heir apparent to a crown. —**crown princess**, the woman or girl next in succession.

crow′s′=nest″, *n.* A masthead shelter for a lookout: usually of barrel form.

cro′zier, ⎰1 krō′zər; 2 erō′zher, *n.* A
cro′sier, ⎱ bishop's official staff upon which is mounted a crook or a cross.

cru′cial, 1 krū′shəl; 2 eru̯′shal, *a.* **1.** Decisive between truth and falsity; critical; searching; as, a *crucial* fact. **2.** Having the form of a cross. —**cru′cial-ly**, *adv.*

cru′ci-ble, 1 krū′sɪ-bl; 2 eru̯′çi-bl, *n.* A pot or vessel made of a substance that will stand extreme heat, for melting metals or minerals.

cru′ci-fix, 1 krū′sɪ-fiks; 2 eru̯′çi-fĭks, *n.* A cross bearing an image of Christ crucified.

cru″ci-fix′ion, 1 krū″sɪ-fik′shən; 2 eru̯″-çi-fĭk′shon, *n.* **1.** The act of putting to death by nailing or binding to a cross. **2.** [**Crucifixion**] Death upon the cross, especially that of Christ on Mount Calvary; also, a statue or picture of that scene.

cru′ci-fy, 1 krū′sɪ-fai; 2 eru̯′çi-fȳ, *vt.* [*cru′ci-fied; cru′ci-fy″ing.*] **1.** To put to death by fastening to a cross. **2.** To subdue, as bodily desires; also, to torture.

crude, 1 krūd; 2 eru̯d, *a.* Not refined; raw; untreated; as, *crude* petroleum. **2.** Unripe; immature. **3.** Lacking in completeness of form or arrangement; as, *crude* ideas. **4.** Characterized by lack of skill; untrained. —**crude′ly**, *adv.* —**crude′ness**, *n.* —**cru′di-ty**, *n.*

cru′el, 1 krū′el; 2 eru̯′ĕl, *a.* **1.** Disposed to inflict suffering; indifferent to others' suffering; as, a *cruel* judge. **2.** Unreasonably severe; harsh. —**cru′el-ly**, *adv.* SYN.: brutal, inhuman, merciless, savage.

cru′el-ty, 1 krū′el-tɪ; 2 eru̯′ĕl-ty, *n.* [*cru′el-ties*, pl.] **1.** The disposition to inflict pain; also, indifference to the suffering of other beings. **2.** A cruel act.

cru′et, 1 krū′et; 2 eru̯′ĕt, *n.* A small glass bottle for vinegar, oil, etc., for table use; a caster.

cruise, 1 krūz; 2 eru̯s, *v.* **I.** *t.* To sail over or through. **II.** *i.* To sail about on the ocean, along a coast, or in the air; generally used of warships, airships, etc.

cruise, *n.* A voyage at sea or in the air.

cruis′er, 1 krūz′ər; 2 eru̯s′er, *n.* **1.** A person, vessel, or vehicle that cruises. **2.** A swift vessel of war with less armor and arms than a battle=ship. **3.** During the 18th century, a privateer; frigate.

crul′ler, 1 krul′ər; 2 erŭl′er, *n.* A ring=shaped cake of dough, fried brown in lard.

crum, ⎰ 1 krum; 2 erŭm. **I.** *vt.* & *vi.*
crumb, ⎱ [*crummed, crumbed; crum′ming, crumb′ing.*] **1.** To break into small pieces; crumble. **2.** In cooking, to dress or cover with bread=crums. **II.** *n.* **1.** A small bit, as of crumbled bread; a fragment; hence, any small amount; as, *crums* of consolation. **2.** The soft inner part of a loaf. —**crum′my**, *a.* **crumb′y** ‡.

crum′ble, 1 krum′bl; 2 erŭm′bl, *vt.* & *vi.* [*crum′bled; crum′bling.*] To cause to fall to pieces; decay; to disintegrate.

crum′bly, 1 krum′blɪ; 2 erŭm′bly, *a.* Apt to crumble; brittle; friable; as, *crumbly* soil.

crum′pet, 1 krum′pet; 2 erŭm′pĕt, *n.* A very thin toasted muffin.

1: ə = final; ɪ = habit; aisle; au = *out*; oil; iū = *feud*; ɔhin; go; н = *loch*; ŋ = si*ng*; thin, this.
2: wǫlf, dǫ; bo͝ok, bo͞ot; fu̯ll, ru̯le, cūre, bŭt, bûrn; ŏil; e = k; ḡo, ḡem; iŋk; ç = s; thin, this.

crum′ple, 1 krŭm′pl; 2 erŭm′pl. **I.** *vt.* & *vi.* [*crum′pled; crum′pling.*] To press into wrinkles; become wrinkled; rumple. **II.** *n.* A wrinkle, as in cloth, or the earth.

crunch, 1 krŭnch; 2 erŭnch. **I.** *vt.* & *vi.* To crush with the teeth, especially with noise; crush or grind noisily; press with crushing force through a brittle substance. **II.** *n.* The act of crunching.

crup′per, 1 krŭp′ər; 2 erŭp′er, *n.* The looped strap that goes under a horse's tail.

cru-sade′, 1 krū-sēd′; 2 erụ-sād′. **I.** *vi.* To go on or engage in a crusade. **II.** *n.* **1.** In history, any of several medieval warlike enterprises of the Christians of Europe, for regaining the Holy Land (1096-1271). **2.** Any vigorous campaign. — **cru-sad′er,** *n.*

cruse, 1 krūs *or* krūz; 2 erụs *or* erụẓ, *n.* A small bottle, flask, or jug; cruet.

crush, 1 krŭsh; 2 erŭsh, *v.* **I.** *t.* To press out of shape; mash; break into bits by pressure; conquer. **II.** *i.* To become broken or misshapen by pressure. — **crush′er,** *n.*

crush, *n.* **1.** A violent colliding; a breaking, bruising, or deforming by violent pressure. **2.** A pressing or crowding together; a crowd.

Crusoe, Robinson. See, *Robinson Crusoe.*

crust, 1 krust; 2 erŭst. **I.** *vt.* & *vi.* To cover with or acquire a crust. **II.** *n.* **1.** A hard, thin coating. **2.** The outer part of bread; a hard or stale piece of bread. **3.** The pastry envelop or cover of a pie.

crus-ta′cean, 1 krus-tē′shan; 2 erŭs-tā′-shan, *n.* One of the large division of jointed-legged animals, called **Crustacea,** lacking a backbone but having a thin, hard, or crust-like shell, as lobsters, crabs, crawfish, etc. — **crus-ta′cean,** *a.* — **crus-ta′-ceous,** 1 krus-tē′shus; 2 erŭs-tā′shŭs, *a.*

crust′y, 1 krust′ı; 2 krŭst′y, *a.* [*crust′i-er; crust′i-est.*] **1.** Crust-like. **2.** Morosely curt in manner or speech; surly; as, a *crusty* old man. — **crust′i-ly,** *adv.* — **crust′i-ness,** *n.*

crutch, 1 krŭch; 2 erŭch, *n.* **1.** A staff with a crosspiece fitting under the armpit, used as a support in walking. **2.** Some similar mechanical device.

crux, 1 kruks; 2 erŭks, *n.* [*crux′es* or *cru′ces,* 1 krū′sīz; 2 erụ′çēs̩, pl.] **1.** A cross. **2.** Anything hard to explain; a puzzle. **3.** The essential question; pivotal point.

cry, 1 krai; 2 erȳ, *v.* [*cried; cry′ing.*] **I.** *t.* To utter loudly and publicly; shout out; proclaim; as, to *cry* goods for sale. **II.** *i.* **1.** To speak, call, or appeal loudly; shout; yell; yelp; bay. **2.** To shed tears; weep. — **to cry down. 1.** To disparage. **2.** To silence or put down by cries. — **to cry up,** to extol.

cry, *n.* [*cries,* pl.] **1.** A loud sound uttered by man or beast, whether in words or not; a call; shout; as, a *cry* of joy, fear, anger; the panther's *cry.* **2.** The act of weeping. **3.** Advertisement by outcry; as, the hawk-

er's *cry.* — **a far cry,** a long way. — **in full cry,** in full pursuit: said of hounds.

cry′ing, 1 krai′ıŋ; 2 erȳ′ing, *pa.* Calling for immediate action; as, a *crying* evil.

crypt, 1 kript; 2 erȳpt, *n.* A recess or vault, as under some churches.

cryp′tic, 1 krip′tık; 2 erȳp′tie, *a.* Secret; occult; hidden; as, a *cryptic* remark. **cryp′-ti-cal** ‡. — **cryp′ti-cal-ly,** *adv.*

crys′tal, 1 kris′təl; 2 erȳs′tal. **I.** *a.* Composed of or like crystal; extremely clear; transparent. **II.** *n.* **1.** The solid geometrical form assumed by many substances, especially minerals. **2.** Colorless transparent quartz. **rock′=crys″tal** ‡. **3.** A watch=glass. **4.** Flint glass.

Snow=crystals.

crys′tal-line, 1 kris′təl-ın *or* -ain; 2 erȳs′tal-in *or* -īn. *a.* **1.** Of, pertaining to, or like crystal. **2.** Transparent; pure.

crys′tal-lize, 1 kris′təl-aiz; 2 erȳs′tal-īz, *v.* [*crys′tal-lized; crys′tal-liz″ing.*] **I.** *t.* To cause to form crystals or become crystalline; bring to definite and permanent form. **II.** *i.* To assume the form of crystals; take on a definite aspect. — **crys′tal-lise** ‡. — **crys′tal-liz″a-ble,** *a.* · **crys″tal-li-za′tion,** *n.*

C. S. Abbreviation of *Christian Science, Civil Service, Confederate States.* — **C. S. A.** Abbreviation of *Confederate States of America.* — **C. S. T.** Abbreviation of *Central Standard Time.* — **Ct.** Abbreviation of *Connecticut, Court.* — **ct.** Abbreviation of *cent, centum* (Latin for 100). — **cts.** Abbreviation of *centimes, cents.* — **cu., cub.** Abbreviations of *cubic.*

cub, 1 kub; 2 eŭb, *n.* **1.** The young of the bear, fox, wolf, and certain other carnivores; a whelp. **2.** A rough, awkward youth.

Cu′ba, 1 kiū′bə; 2 eū′ba, *n.* A republic (44,164 square miles); the largest island in the West Indies; capital, Havana. — **Cu′ban,** *a.* & *n.*

cube, 1 kiūb; 2 eūb. **I.** *vt.* [*cubed; cub′ing.*] **1.** To shape or cut into a cube. **2.** To find the cubic capacity of. **II.** *n.* A solid having six equal square sides and all its angles right angles.

cu′bic, 1 kiū′bık; 2 eū′bic, *a.* **1.** Formed like a cube. **2.** Being, or equal to, a cube whose edge is a given unit; as, a *cubic* foot. **cu′bi-cal** ‡. — **cu′bi-cal-ly,** *adv.*

cu′bit, 1 kiū′bıt; 2 eū′bit, *n.* An ancient measure of length; the length of the forearm: about 18 to 20 inches.

cuck′oo, 1 kuk′ū; 2 eụk′ōō. **I.** *vi.* [*cuck′-*

ooed; *cuck'oo-ing*.] To utter or imitate the cry of the cuckoo. **II.** *n*. **1.** A bird with a two=toned cry, many species of which, as the common European cuckoo, deposit their eggs to be hatched in the nests of other birds. **2.** Any of various birds with cries similar to the English cuckoo, as the American **yellow= billed cuckoo** and the **black=billed cuckoo**, which hatch their own eggs. **3.** A cuckoo's cry. — **cuck'oo**, *a*.

Cuckoo (1).

cu'cum-ber, 1kiū'-kum-bər; 2 eū'eŭm-ber, *n*. **1.** The oblong fruit of a creeping plant of the gourd family, used in making salads and for pickles. **2.** The plant itself.

cud, 1 kud; 2 eŭd, *n*. The food forced up into the mouth from the first stomach of a ruminant and chewed again.

cud'dle, 1 kud'l; 2 eŭd'l, *v*. [*cud'dled; cud'dling*.] **1.** *t*. To protect and caress within a close embrace; hug. **II.** *i*. To lie close; hug one another. **III.** *n*. An embrace; caress.

cudg'el, 1 kuj'el; 2 eŭdg'ĕl. **I.** *vt*. [*cudg'eled* or *cudg'elled; cudg'el-ing* or *cudg'el-ling*.] To beat with a cudgel. **II.** *n*. A short thick stick used as a club. — **to cudgel one's brains,** to think hard. — **to take up the cudgels,** to enter into a contest.

cue, 1 kiū; 2 eū, *n*. **1.** A tail, or tail=like appendage; as: (1) A long braid of hair. (2) A line of people waiting to buy tickets. **queue** ‡. **2.** The closing words of an actor's speech serving as a signal for the actor following. **3.** A hint; suggestion. **4.** A straight tapering stick, used in playing billiards.

cuff, 1 kuf; 2 eŭf, *vt*. To strike, as with the open hand; to beat.

cuff [1], *n*. A blow with the unclosed hand.

cuff [2], *n*. **1.** A band about the wrist. **2.** The lower part of a sleeve. **3.** The bottom part of a trouser=leg folded back. **4.** The part of a long glove covering the wrist.

cui-rass', 1 kwĭ-ras'; 2 ewĭ-răs', *n*. **1.** A piece of armor covering the upper part of the trunk and consisting of a breastplate and a back=plate. **2.** The breastplate alone.

cui-sine', 1 kwĭ-zēn'; 2 ewĭ-şĭn', *n*. The kitchen; cooking department; also, the style or quality of cooking.

cu'li-na-ry, 1 kiū'lɪ-nār-ɪ; 2 eū'li-nâr-y, *a*. Of or pertaining to cooking or the kitchen.

cull, 1 kul; 2 eŭl. **I.** *vt*. [*culled; cull'ing*.] **1.** To pick or sort out. **2.** To select and gather. **II.** *n*. Something picked or sorted out; also, something rejected. — **cull'er,** *n*.

culm, 1 kulm; 2 eŭlm, *n*. In botany, the jointed, usually hollow, stem of a grass.

cul'mi-nate, 1 kul'mɪ-nēt; 2 eŭl'mi-nāt, *vi*. [*cul'mi-nat"ed; cul'mi-nat"ing*.] **1.** To attain the highest point or degree. **2.** To come to a complete result; reach a final effect. — **cul"mi-na'tion,** *n*.

cul'pa-ble, 1 kul'pə-bl; 2 eŭl'pa-bl, *a*. Deserving of blame or censure; guilty. — **cul"pa-bil'i-ty,** *n*. — **cul'pa-bly,** *adv*.

SYN.: criminal, faulty, reprehensible, wicked.

cul'prit, 1 kul'prɪt; 2 eŭl'prit, *n*. **1.** A guilty person; criminal; an offender. **2.** Formerly, one charged with a crime but not yet convicted.

cult, 1 kult; 2 eŭlt, *n*. **1.** Worship or religious devotion; especially, the forms of a religion. **2.** A system of religious observances. **3.** Devotion to an idea, theory, thing, or person; as, the Browning *cult*; also, the object of such devotion, or the group showing the devotion.

cul'ti-vate, 1 kul'tɪ-vēt; 2 eŭl'ti-vāt, *vt*. [*cul'ti-vat"ed; cul'ti-vat"ing*.] **1.** To work by stirring, fertilizing, sowing, and reaping; to raise crops from. **2.** To loosen the soil about growing plants with a plow or cultivator; as, to *cultivate* potatoes twice. **3.** To improve or develop by study, exercise, or training; refine; civilize. **4.** To pay close attention to. — **cul"ti-va'tion,** *n*.

cul'ti-va"tor, 1 kul'tɪ-vē"tər; 2 eŭl'ti-vā"-tor, *n*. **1.** A person who cultivates. **2.** A machine for cultivating: usually having several shares, blades, or disks which loosen the ground and destroy weeds.

cul'ture, 1 kul'-ćhur *or* -tiur; 2 eŭl'chur *or* -tūr, *n*. **1.** The cultivation of plants or animals, especially with a view to improvement; as, bee=*culture*. **2.** The training, improvement, and refinement of mind, morals, or taste. **3.** Tillage of the soil. **4.** Enlightenment or civilization. — **cul'tur-al,** *a*. — **cul'tured,** *pa*. — **cul'tur-ist,** *n*.

Cultivator (2).

SYN.: breeding, education, learning, polish.

cul'vert, 1 kul'-vərt; 2 eŭl'vert, *n*. An artificial covered channel or drain crossing underneath a road, canal, railroad, or the like.

Culvert.

cum'ber, 1 kum'bər; 2 eŭm'ber, *vt*. To hinder by a weight or burden; hamper.

cum'ber-some, 1 kum'bər-səm; 2 eŭm'-

ber-som, *a.* Moving or working heavily or with difficulty; unwieldy; troublesome; burdensome. —**cum′ber-some-ly,** *adv.* —**cum′ber-some-ness,** *n.*

cum′brous, 1 kŭm′brus; 2 eŭm′brŭs, *a.* Cumbersome. —**cum′brous-ly,** *adv.*

cu′mu-la-tive, 1 kiū′miu-lə-tĭv; 2 eū′-mū-la-tiv, *a.* Gathering volume, strength, or value by successive addition.

cu′ne-i-form, 1 kiū′nĭ-[*or* kiu-nĭ′]ĭ-fôrm; 2 eū′ne-[*or* eū-ne′]i-fôrm. *a.* Wedge=shaped, as the characters in ancient Assyrian inscriptions.

cun′ning, 1 kŭn′ɪŋ; 2 eŭn′ing, *a.* **1.** Crafty or shrewd; deceitful; sly; as, a *cunning* fox. **2.** Dexterous; skilful; as, a *cunning* carpenter. **3.** In common speech, bright; amusing; cute. —**cun′ning-ly,** *adv.*

cun′ning, *n.* **1.** A crafty disposition; guile; as, the *cunning* of a low rogue. **2.** Knowledge combined with skill.

cup, 1 kŭp; 2 eŭp. **I.** *vt. & vi.* [*cupped; cup′ping.*] **1.** To be or become cup=shaped; make in the shape of a cup. **2.** To place in a cup. **II.** *n.* **1.** A small drinking=vessel. **2.** A cupful. **3.** Any cup=shaped object; as, the *cup* of an acorn or a flower; an oil=*cup.* —**in his cups,** intoxicated; also, in the act of drinking.

cup′bear″er, *n.* One who serves the cups of drink, as to guests at a feast.

cup′board, 1 kŭb′ərd; 2 eŭb′ord, *n.* **1.** A closet or cabinet with shelves for keeping food, dishes, etc. **2.** Any small closet.

cup′ful, 1 kŭp′ful; 2 eŭp′fŭl, *n.* [*cup′fuls,* pl.] The amount a cup will hold.

Cu′pid, 1 kiū′pɪd; 2 eū′pid, *n.* In Roman mythology, the god of love; the Greek *Eros.*

cu-pid′i-ty, 1 kiu-pĭd′ɪ-tɪ; 2 eū-pĭd′i-ty, *n.* An excessive desire for possession, especially of wealth; avarice.

cu′po-la, 1 kiū′po-lə; 2 eū′po-la, *n.* **1.** A roof shaped like a dome. **2.** The ceiling or concave interior of a dome. **3.** A revolving dome=shaped protection within which the guns of a ship or fort are worked.

cur, 1 kur; 2 eŭr, *n.* **1.** A mongrel, worthless dog. **2.** A mean, malicious, or cowardly person. —**cur′rish,** *a.* —**cur′rish-ly,** *adv.*

cur′a-ble, 1 kiūr′ə-bl; 2 eūr′a-bl, *a.* Able to be cured.

cu′rate, 1 kiū′rɪt; 2 eū′rat, *n.* A clergyman appointed to assist a vicar, rector, pastor, or priest.

cur′a-tive, 1 kiūr′ə-tɪv; 2 eūr′a-tiv. **I.** *a.* Having power or tendency to cure. **II.** *n.* A remedy.

cu-ra′tor, 1 kiu-rē′tər; 2 eū-rā′tor, *n.* A person having charge or oversight, as of a museum or library; a custodian.

curb, 1 kurb; 2 eŭrb. **I.** *vt. & vi.* **1.** To check or control, as with reins and curb. **2.** To protect by a curb. **II.** *n.* **1.** A chain or strap attached under the lower jaw to a bit to secure greater control over a horse. **2.** Anything that controls or restrains. **3.** A curbstone or a line of curbstones at the outer edge of a sidewalk. **4.** A framework at the top of a well.

SYN.: bridle, govern, hinder, repress, subdue.

curd, 1 kurd; 2 eŭrd. **I.** *vt. & vi.* To cover with curd; also, to curdle. **II.** *n.* The thick or clotted portion of milk of which cheese is made. —**curd′y,** *a.*

cur′dle, 1 kur′dl; 2 eŭr′dl, *v.* [*cur′dled; cur′dling.*] **I.** *t.* To change into curd; cause to thicken; as, acids *curdle* milk. **II.** *i.* To turn to curd; grow thick. —**curd′ly,** *a.*

cure, kiūr; 2 eūr, *v.* [*cured; cur′ing.*] **I.** *t.* **1.** To restore to a healthy or sound condition. **2.** To free from disease or evil; heal. **3.** To preserve, as by salting, drying, or smoking; as, to *cure* hams. **4.** To vulcanize; as, to *cure* rubber. **II.** *i.* **1.** To bring about recovery, as from disease. **2.** To be preserved by salting or smoking.

cure, *n.* **1.** The act of restoring to a sound or healthy condition. **2.** That which restores health or abolishes an evil. **3.** A method of curing anything, as ham. —**cure′all″,** *n.* A panacea.

cu-ré′, 1 kiu-rē′ *or* (F.) kü″rē′; 2 eū-rę′ *or* (F.) eü″rę′, *n.* A French parish priest of the Roman Catholic Church.

cur′few, 1 kur′fiū; 2 eŭr′fū, *n.* **1.** An ancient police order that all fires and lights be put out at a certain fixed time in the evening at the tolling of a bell; also, the bell itself, its sound, or the time of ringing. **2.** The ringing of a bell at a set time in the evening to warn children off the streets.

cu′ri-o, 1 kiū′rɪ-o; 2 eū′ri-o, *n.* A curiosity; an odd, rare article.

cu″ri-os′i-ty, 1 kiū″rɪ-ŏs′ɪ-tɪ; 2 eū″ri-ŏs′i-ty, *n.* [*cu″ri-os′i-ties,* pl.] **1.** A desire for knowledge of something, as the private affairs of others. **2.** An unusual object.

cu′ri-ous, 1 kiū′rɪ-us; 2 eū′ri-ŭs, *a.* **1.** Eager for information; inquisitive; as, many questions were asked by the *curious* boy. **2.** Attracting attention; novel; odd; strange; mysterious; as, *curious* pieces of china. —**cu′ri-ous-ly,** *adv.* —**cu′ri-ous-ness,** *n.*

SYN.: interesting, odd, prying, singular.

curl, 1 kurl; 2 eŭrl, *v.* **I.** *t.* **1.** To coil (the hair) into ringlets, curves, or spirals. **2.** To adorn with curls. **II.** *i.* To become curled; take spiral shape; as, in autumn the leaves *curl.* —**curl′er,** *n.*

curl, *n.* **1.** Anything coiled or spiral, as a ringlet of hair. **2.** A wavy or circling mark. —**curl′i-ness,** *n.*

cur'lew, 1 kūr'liū; 2 eûr'lū, *n.* A shore-bird of large size, having a long, curved bill and long legs.

Curlew.

curl'y, 1 kūrl'ı; 2 eûrl'y, *a.* [*curl'i-er; curl'i-est.*] Having curls or coils; wavy; as, she had *curly* hair.

cur-mud'geon, 1 kər-muj'ən; 2 eur-mŭdg'on, *n.* A miserly or surly person.

cur'rant, 1 kur'ənt; 2 eŭr'ant, *n.* A small, round, acid berry, either red or black, used in making preserves, jellies, and jams; also, the bush producing it.

cur'ren-cy, 1 kur'ən-sı; 2 eŭr'en-çy, *n.* [*cur'ren-cies,* pl.] **1.** The money in use in a country for buying and selling; coins, government bills, or bank-notes. **2.** The state of being current; as, the *currency* of a rumor. **3.** Current value or estimation; general esteem or standing; as, to gain *currency* without merit.

cur'rent, 1 kur'ent; 2 eŭr'ĕnt. **I.** *a.* **1.** Circulating freely. **2.** Generally accepted. in common use; as, *current* styles or fashions. **3.** In actual progress, or belonging to the immediate present; as; the *current* issue of a magazine. **II.** *n.* **1.** A continuous flow of air or water in a definite direction, especially through a slower moving body; as, to swim against the *current* of a stream. **2.** Electricity flowing along a cable or wire. **3.** Any connected onward movement. —**cur'rent-ly,** *adv.*

cur-ric'u-lum, 1 ku-rik'yu-lum; 2 eŭ-rĭe'yu-lŭm, *n.* [*cur-ric'u-lums* or *cur-ric'u-la,* pl.] A course of study in a school.

cur'ry, 1 kur'ı; 2 eŭr'y, *vt.* [*cur'ried; cur'ry-ing.*] **1.** To clean with a currycomb. **2.** To dress for use by soaking, scouring, smoothing, coloring, etc.: said of tanned hides. —**to curry favor,** to seek favor by flattery and servility.

cur'ry, *n.* [*cur'ries,* pl.] **1.** A pungent sauce, of East-Indian origin, used as a relish for boiled rice, meats, etc. **curry sauce** ‡. **2.** A dish of food served with this sauce.

cur'ry-comb″, 1 kur'ı-kōm″; 2 eŭr'y-eōm″, *n.* A comb made up of several rows of notched edges or teeth, used for cleaning horses and cattle.

Currycomb.

curse, 1 kūrs; 2 eûrs, *v.* [*cursed* or *curst; curs'ing.*] **I.** *t.* **1.** To call evil upon; execrate. **2.** To swear at. **3.** To cause great evils to; harass; torment. **II.** *i.* To swear; blaspheme.

curse, *n.* **1.** A plea or wish for harm or evil to fall upon a person; any profane oath; as, *curses* loud and deep. **2.** Evil or misfortune invoked or threatened; as, a *curse* is upon that man. **3.** A source of disaster; that which brings evil; as, war is a *curse.* **4.** Something accursed.

curs'ed, 1 kūrs'ed or kūrst; 2 eûrs'ĕd or eûrst, *a.* **1.** Under a curse. **2.** Deserving a curse; detestable; wicked. —**curs'ed-ly,** *adv.*

cur'so-ry, 1 kūr'so-rı; 2 eûr'so-ry, *a.* Rapid and slight; hasty; not thorough; as, he made a *cursory* examination of the ship. —**cur'so-ri-ly,** *adv.* —**cur'so-ri-ness,** *n.*

Syn.: careless, heedless, loose, superficial.

curt, 1 kūrt; 2 eûrt, *a.* Brief and abrupt; short and sharp in manner; as, to give a *curt* answer. —**curt'ly,** *adv.* —**curt'ness,** *n.*

Syn.: blunt, brusk, concise, rude, terse.

cur-tail', 1 kər-tēl'; 2 eur-tāl', *vt.* To cut off, or cut short; lessen; reduce; as, to *curtail* expenses. —**cur-tail'ment,** *n.*

Syn.: decrease, diminish, economize, retrench.

cur'tain, 1 kūr'tın; 2 eûr'tin. **I.** *vt.* To supply with curtains; separate as by a curtain. **II.** *n.* **1.** An adjustable draping or covering, hanging loosely. **2.** Something that conceals or separates.

curt'sy, kūrt'sı; 2 eûrt'sy. **I.** *vi.* [*curt'sied; curt'sy-ing.*] To make a curtsy. **II.** *n.* [*curt'sies,* pl.] A downward movement of the body made by bending the knees. Preferred form of *courtesy.* **court'sey** ‡; **curt'sey** ‡.

cur'va-ture, 1 kūr'və-ĉhur or -tiur; 2 eûr'va-chụr or -tūr, *n.* **1.** The act of bending, or the state of being bent; a curving. **2.** Something curved or bent.

curve, 1 kūrv; 2 eûrv. **I.** *vt. & vi.* [*curved; curv'ing.*] **1.** To have or cause to take the form of a curve. **2.** To move in a curve; as, the ball *curved.* **II.** *a.* Having a different direction at every point; as, a *curve* line or surface. **III.** *n.* **1.** A line continuously bent so that no part of it is straight, as the arc of a circle. **2.** A bending or something bent; as, a railway *curve.* **3.** In baseball, the bend produced by the pitcher in the path of the ball.

cur'vet, 1 kūr'vet or kər-vet'; 2 eûr'vĕt or eur-vĕt', *v.* [*cur'vet-ed* or *cur'vet-ted; cur'vet-ing* or *cur'vet-ting.*] **I.** *vt. & vi.* To prance or cause to prance. **II.** *n.* A low leap of a horse made by raising and advancing first the fore legs and then, as they begin to fall, raising the hind legs so that at one time all four legs are off the ground.

cush'ion, 1 kush'ən; 2 eush'on. **I.** *vt.* **1.** To place on a cushion. **2.** To provide with a cushion. **II.** *n.* **1.** A flexible bag or casing filled with some soft or elastic material such as feathers or air. **2.** Anything like a cushion, especially a device to deaden noise or shock.

cusp, 1 kᴜsp; 2 eŭsp, *n.* **1.** A point, as on the crown of a tooth. **2.** One of the points of a crescent moon, or something resembling it. —**cusped,** *a.*

cus'pi-dor, 1 kᴜs'pı-dŏr; 2 eŭs'pi-dôr, *n.* A spittoon.

cus'tard, 1 kᴜs'tərd; 2 eŭs'tard, *n.* A mixture of eggs, milk, sugar, etc., boiled or baked.

cus-to'di-an, 1 kᴜs-tō'dı-ən; 2 eŭs-tō'di-an, *n.* A caretaker of something.

cus'to-dy, 1 kᴜs'to-dı; 2 eŭs'to-dy, *n.* **1.** A keeping; watch; care; as, the town clerk had the *custody* of the public records. **2.** Under arrest; imprisonment; as, the burglar was taken into *custody*.

cus'tom, 1 kᴜs'təm; 2 eŭs'tom, *a.* **1.** Made or done upon a customer's order; as, a *custom* overcoat. **2.** Making or doing things upon an order; as a *custom* tailor; a *custom* shoemaker.

cus'tom, *n.* **1.** An ordinary or usual manner of doing or acting. **2.** The habitual practise of a community or country. **3.** Business support; regular trade; as, low prices draw *custom*. **4.** [**customs**] A duty imposed by law on goods imported.

Sʏɴ.: fashion, rule, style, use.

cus'tom-a-ry, 1 kᴜs'təm-ār-ı; 2 eŭs'-tom-âr-y, *a.* Conforming to or established by custom; usual. —**cus'tom-a-ri-ly,** *adv.*

cus'tom-er, 1 kᴜs'təm-ər; 2 eŭs'tom-er, *n.* One who gives his custom or trade; a purchaser.

cus'tom=house", *n.* The place where entries of imports are made and duties collected.

cut, 1 kᴜt; 2 eŭt, *v.* [*cut; cut'ting.*] **I.** *t.* **1.** To make a gash in, by means of a sharp edge; wound with or as with an edged tool. **2.** Affect deeply; hurt; as, her indifference *cuts* me to the heart. **3.** To pass through like a blade; as, to *cut* water with an oar. **4.** To divide or sever with a sharp tool; as, to *cut* bread. **5.** To make, prepare, or shape with a sharp tool; as, to *cut* one's nails. **6.** To cross or intersect; as, one line *cuts* another. **7.** To reduce the length or extent of; shorten; as, to *cut* the film to a short comedy. **8.** To pretend not to know; ignore; as, to *cut* a former friend. **9.** To stay away from; as, to *cut* a class. **10.** In cards, to divide (the pack) to determine a trump or to prevent cheating. **11.** In tennis, to give a spinning motion to (a ball). **II.** *i.* **1.** To operate, make, or act by cutting. **2.** To be adapted for cutting.

cut, *n.* **1.** The opening, cleft, or wound made by an edged instrument; a gash; a slit. **2.** A cutting motion or stroke. **3.**

The part cut off; as, a *cut* of meat. **4.** That which cuts or hurts the feelings. **5.** A cutting; as, a railway *cut* through a hill. **6.** A direct way, as across an angle. **7.** Fashion, form, style; as, the *cut* of a suit. **8.** In printing, an engraved block, or an impression from it. **9.** A reduction in prices or rates; as, a *cut* in pay. **10.** A deliberate absence from lectures or classes.

cute, 1 kiūt; 2 eūt, *a.* **1.** Clever and sharp; shrewd; as, a *cute* trick. **2.** Bright and taking; attractive; as, a *cute* baby. —**cute'-ly,** *adv.* —**cute'ness,** *n.*

cu'ti-cle, 1 kiū'tı-kl; 2 eū'ti-el, *n.* **1.** In anatomy, the outer layer of cells that protects the true skin; the epidermis; scarf=skin. **2.** The old skin at the sides and bottom of a fingernail.

cut'las, 1 kᴜt'ləs; 2 eŭt'las, *n.* [*cut'las-es,* pl.] A short heavy sword=like weapon, used mainly in naval hand=to=hand combat. **cut'lass ‡.**

Cutlases.

1. English cutlas of the 15th century. 2. German cutlas of the 15th century. 3. Mariners' saw=edged cutlas of the 17th century.

cut'ler, 1 kᴜt'lər; 2 eŭt'ler, *n.* One who makes, repairs, or deals in cutlery.

cut'ler-y, 1 kᴜt'lər-ı; 2 eŭt'ler-y, *n.* Cutting instruments collectively, as knives, scissors, shears, razors, etc.; especially the ones used for cutting and eating food.

cut'let, 1 kᴜt'let; 2 eŭt'lĕt, *n.* **1.** A thin piece of meat, as veal or mutton, for frying or broiling. **2.** A portion of fish, chopped meat, or other food, in the form of a cutlet.

cut'=off", *n.* **1.** A short cut, as in a roadway, railway, river, etc., that has been straightened and the length reduced. **2.** A mechanism that cuts off flow, as of steam or water. **3.** The point at which the flow is thus cut off. —**cut'=out",** *n.* Something to be cut out, as a picture, pattern, or design. —**cut'purse",** *n.* A pickpocket.

cut'ter, 1 kᴜt'ər; 2 eŭt'er, *n.* **1.** One who cuts, shapes, or fits anything by cutting. **2.** That which cuts, as a tool or machine; as, a paper=*cutter*. **3.** A small, swift, armed ship used by the United States coast guard service. **4.** A sharp single=masted vessel rigged like a sloop. **5.** A medium=sized boat carried by a battle=ship. **6.** In North America, a small sleigh.

cut'throat". **I.** *a.* Villainous; murderous; destructive; as, *cutthroat* competition in business. **II.** *n.* A murderer.

cut′ting, 1 kut′ɪŋ; 2 eŭt′ing. **I.** *pa.* **1.** Adapted to cut; edged; as, the *cutting* edge of an instrument. **2.** Disagreeably penetrating; sharp; chilling; as, *cutting* breezes. **3.** Tending to wound the feelings; sarcastic; caustic; as, *cutting* remarks. **II.** *n.* **1.** The act of severing. **2.** Something obtained or made by cutting; a piece cut off or out.

cut′tle-bone″, 1 kut′l-bōn″; 2 eŭt′l-bōn″, *n.* The internal, bony plate of a cuttlefish, used as a relish for caged birds, and for polishing metals.

cut′tle-fish″, 1 kut′l-fish″; 2 eŭt′l-fish″, *n.* [*cut′tle-fish″* or *cut′tle-fish″es,* pl.] A greedy, flesh=eating, marine mollusk with 8 or 10 sucker=bearing arms and an internal, bony plate. It has the power of ejecting a black, inky fluid, the sepia, to conceal itself.

Cuttlefish.

cut′worm″, *n.* A destructive caterpillar that cuts off young plants close to the ground, or that destroys buds on trees.

cy-ber-net′ics, 1 sai-bər′net-iks; 2 çў-ber′nĕt-ĭes, *n.* The science which deals with the principles of control and communication in machines and organisms.—**cyber-net′tic** *a.*

cyc′la-men, 1 sik′lə-men; 2 çўe′la-mĕn, *n.* A bulbous herb of the primrose family, with large heart=shaped leaves, and tall slender stalks, each bearing a single drooping flower. **sow′bread″** ‡.

cy′cle, 1 sai′kl; 2 çў′el, *vi.* [*cy′cled; cy′cling.*] To ride a bicycle or tricycle.

cy′cle, *n.* **1.** A period of time, at the end of which certain aspects or motions of the heavenly bodies repeat themselves; as, lunar *cycles.* **2.** A round of years or of ages; a vast period; an eon. **3.** A body of legends relating to some period, person, etc. **4.** A bicycle or tricycle.

Cyclamen.
a, flower; *b,* cordate leaves.

cyc′lic, 1 sik′lɪk or sai′klɪk; 2 çўe′lie or çў′elie, *a.* Having or pertaining to a cycle; recurring in cycles. **cyc′li-cal** ‡.

cy′clist, 1 sai′klist; 2 çў′elĭst, *n.* One who rides a bicycle, tricycle, motor=cycle, etc.

cy′clone, 1 sai′klōn; 2 çў′elŏn, *n.* A violent and destructive wind=storm with winds blowing spirally about a center of low pressure; a tornado. — **cy-clon′ic,** *a.*

Cy″clo-pe′an, 1 sai″klo-pī′ən; 2 çў″elo-pē′an, *a.* Of or pertaining to the Cyclopes or their work; gigantic; colossal.

cy″clo-pe′di-a, ⎰ 1 sai″klo-pī′dɪ-a; 2 çў″-
cy″clo-pæ′di-a, ⎱ elo-pē′di-a, *n.* An encyclopedia. — **cy″clo-pe′dic,** *a.*

Cy′clops, 1 sai′klɒps; 2 çў′elŏps, *n.* [*Cy′-clo-pes* or *Cy-clops,* pl.] In Homeric legend, one of a race of one=eyed giants in Sicily.

cy′clo-tron, 1 sai′klo-tron; 2 eў′klo-trŏn, *n.* An atom smasher.

cyg′net, 1 sig′net; 2 çўg′nĕt, *n.* A young swan.

cyl′in-der, 1 sil′ɪn-dər; 2 çўl′in-der, *n.* **1.** A circular body, solid or hollow, shaped like a roller. **2.** Any part of a machine in the form of a cylinder, usually hollow; as, the *cylinder* of a steam=engine or of a printing=press.—**cy-lin′dri-cal,** *a.* **cy-lin′dric** ‡. —**cy-lin′dri-cal-ly,** *adv.*

cym′bal, 1 sim′bəl; 2 çўm′-bal, *n.* One of a pair of plate-like, metallic, musical instruments played by being clashed together.

Cymbals.

cyn′ic, 1 sin′ɪk; 2 eўn′ie, *n.* A sneering, critical person; one who hates his fellow men. —**cyn′ic,** *a.* **cyn′i-cal** ‡.—**cyn′i-cism,** *n.*

cy′no-sure, 1 sai′no-[or sin′o-]shur; 2 çў′-no-[or eўn′o-]shur, *n.* An object of general interest or attention.

cy′press, 1 sai′pres; 2 çў′prĕs, *n.* **1.** Any one of several evergreen trees of the pine family. **2.** The timber of the cypress.

Cy′prus, 1 sai′prus; 2 çў′prŭs, *n.* A British island (3,584 square miles) in the Mediterranean Sea.

Cy′rus, 1 sai′rus; 2 çў′rŭs, *n.* "The Great," founder of the Persian Empire.

cyst, 1 sist; 2 çўst, *n.* A small closed sac or bag containing diseased, fluid matter.

cy′to″plasm, 1 sai′to-plazm; 2 çў′to-plaşm, *n.* All the protoplasm of the cell except that in the nucleus.—**cy″to-plas′-mic** *a.*

czar, 1 zār; 2 zär, *n.* An emperor or absolute monarch; supreme lord; specifically [*Czar*], one of the former rulers of Russia.

Czech, 1 ćhek; 2 ćhĕe, *n.* **1.** A member of that branch of the Slavic people of Bohemia, Moravia, and Hungary. **2.** The language of the Czechs. **Czech″o=Slo′vak** ‡.

Czech″o=Slo-vak′i-a, 1 ćhek″o=slo-vak′-1-ə; 2 ćhĕe″o=slo-väk′i-a, *n.* A west central European republic; partitioned among Germany, Hungary, and Poland, 1938-1939, with the exception of a part of Slovakia, a republic under German rule, 1939; reconstituted, 1945; capital, Praha (Prague); 49.330 square miles. **Czech″o-slo-vak′i-a** ‡.

D

D, d, 1 dī; 2 dē, *n.* [*dees*, *D's*, or *Ds*, pl.] **1.** The fourth letter in the English alphabet. **2.** As a symbol, it denotes the fourth in a series or class. **3.** As a Roman numeral, D stands for 500. **4.** In music, the second note in the scale of C major.
d. Abbreviation of *denarius* (Latin for *penny*, *pence*), *dollar*.

dab, 1 dab; 2 dăb, *vt.* & *vi.* [*dabbed*; *dab'bing*.] To strike softly or quickly; pat.

dab, *n.* **1.** A gentle blow; a pat. **2.** A small lump of soft substance, as butter.

dab'ble, 1 dab'l; 2 dăb'l, *v.* [*dab'bled*; *dab'bling*.] **I.** *t.* To dip lightly and often; splash; sprinkle; as, to *dabble* flowers with water. **II.** *i.* **1.** To play, as with the hands, in a fluid; splash gently. **2.** To take a slight or superficial interest in something. —**dab'bler,** *n.*

Dace.

dace, 1 dēs; 2 dāç, *n.* [*dac'es* or *dace*, pl.] A small fresh=water fish.

dachs'hund, 1 dūнs'hunt *or* daks'hund; 2 däнs'hụnt *or* dăes'hụnd, *n.* A small, short=haired dog with a long body and short legs. See *dog*.

dad, 1 dad; 2 dăd, *n.* Another name for father: used familiarly. **dad'da** ‡; **dad'die** ‡; **dad'dy** ‡ [*dad'dies*, pl.].

dad'dy=long'=legs", 1 dad'ı=lŏŋ'=legz"; 2 dăd'y=lông'=lĕg̣s", *n.* A spiderlike insect having a small, roundish body and very long, slender legs.

daf'fo-dil, 1 daf'o-dil; 2 dăf'o-dĭl, *n.* A plant about one foot tall, growing from a bulb, with 4 to 6 slender, flat, erect leaves. The flower=stems bear a single, yellow, trumpet=like blossom about 2 inches long. **daf'fy-down-dil"ly** ‡.

daft, 1 daft; 2 dȧft, *a.* Silly; insane; imbecile.

Daffodil.
a, flower; *b*, linear leaves.

dag'ger, 1 dag'ər; 2 dăg'er, *n.* **1.** A short, edged and pointed weapon, for stabbing, etc. **2.** In printing, a reference=mark (†). — **double dagger,** a mark of reference (‡) used in printing.

dah'lia, 1 dāl'yə *or* dē'lyə; 2 dăl'ya *or* dā'lyȧ, *n.* **1.** A genus of tall, many=branched, flowering herbs, growing from clusters of tubers,

Daggers (1).

and bearing many large heads of ray=shaped flowers in shades of red and other colors. **2.** A plant, tuber, or flower of this genus.

Dahlia.

dai'ly, 1 dē'lı; 2 dā'ly. **I.** *a.* Occurring, appearing, or pertaining to every day; as, *daily* exercise. **II.** *n.* [*dai'lies*, pl.] A daily publication. **III.** *adv.* Day after day; on every day.

dain'ty, 1 dēn'tı; 2 dān'ty. **I.** *a.* [*dain'ti-er*; *dain'ti-est*.] **1.** Refined or particular in taste; as, a *dainty* appetite; also, overnice. **2.** Delicate and agreeable to the taste; delicious; as, a *dainty* cake. **3.** Delicate and elegant in appearance. **II.** *n.* [*dain'ties*, pl.] Something choice, delicate, or delicious. — **dain'ti-ly,** *adv.* —**dain'ti-ness,** *n.*

dair'y, 1 dār'ı; 2 dâr'y, *n.* [*dai'ries*, pl.] **1.** A place where milk is kept and made into butter and cheese. **2.** A place for the sale of milk=products; a dairy=farm. **3.** The business of dealing in such products. — **dair'y=cat"tle,** *n. pl.* — **dair'y=farm",** *n.* — **dair'y=maid",** *n.* — **dair'y=man",** *n.* — **dair'y=wo"man,** *n.* —**dair'y-ing,** *n.*

da'is, 1 dē'ıs; 2 dā'ıs, *n.* A raised platform in a large room or hall.

dai'sy, 1 dē'zı; 2 dā'g̣y, *n.* [*dai'sies*, pl.] **1.** A low herb whose flowers have a yellow center with white or rose=colored petals. **2.** The flower itself.

dale, 1 dēl; 2 dāl, *n.* A small valley.

dal'li-ance, 1 dal'ı-əns; 2 dăl'i-ȧnç, *n.* The act of dallying, loitering, or fondling.

dal'ly, 1 dal'ı; 2 dăl'y, *vi.* [*dal'lied*; *dal'ly-ing*.] To trifle away time; toy; loiter; delay.

Dal-ma'tia, 1 dal-mē'şhə; 2 dăl-mā'sha, *n.* A region of Yugoslavia on the east coast of the Adriatic Sea. — **Dal-ma'tian,** *a.* & *n.* — **Dalmatian (dog),** a coach dog.

dam, 1 dam; 2 dăm, *vt.* [*dammed*; *dam'ming*.] To stop or obstruct by a dam; restrain; as, to *dam* a river.

dam^1, *n.* **1.** A barrier to stop the flow of a stream. **2.** The water held up by a dam.

dam^2, *n.* A female parent: now used chiefly of domestic animals.

dam'age, 1 dam'ıj; 2 dăm'ȧj. **I.** *vt.* & *vi.* [*dam'aged*; *dam'ag-ing*.] To harm; injure; impair; as, to *damage* a car; to become injured or impaired. **II.** *n.* **1.** Injury; harm; as, *damage* from a storm. **2.** [pl.] In law, money recoverable for an injury or wrong.

1: ȧrtistic, ärt; fat, fāre; fast; get, prēy; hit, police; obey, gō; net, ēr; full, rūle; but, būrn;
2: ärt, āpe, făt, fâre, fȧst, sofa; mē, gĕt, prẹy, fêrn, over; hi̇t, ice; ı̆ =ē; ĭ = ĕ; gō, nŏt, ôr, wȯn,

(Continued in Volume Six)

INSECTS

Illustrated by Sy Barlowe

American Locust

A champion long-distance jumper is the familiar Locust of our fields and meadows. It is quite often considered a serious pest as it will eat almost any kind of plant, and that doesn't make it too popular with Farmer Jones.

Mrs. Locust lays her eggs underground in the spring and they hatch into what are called "nymphs." These "nymphs," or baby Locusts, look like their mothers but do not have wings. They shed their skins about 5 times before they become full-grown adults.

When the area in which the Locusts are living cannot accommodate their increasing population, they swarm in countless numbers and fly to other places eating large amounts of plants and crops on their destructive way.

True Size

Ant Lion

It is hard to imagine that the harmless, slender, gauzy-winged adult Ant Lion is in any way connected with its fierce larvae.

The female lays her eggs on the ground. When they hatch, the larva burrows into the sandy soil, making a pitfall to trap any unwary ants that may fall in. When an ant, or other wingless creature, comes up to the edge of the pit, the sand crumbles under its feet and it tumbles into the powerful jaws of the waiting Ant Lion larva lying buried at the bottom. Once its prey is in its grasp, the Ant Lion's jaws never let go for a moment until the victim is sucked dry of body juices.

The jaws of the larva are hollow, and made for sucking as well as grasping.

It may take from 1 to 3 years for the larva to mature. As it grows it builds a globular silken cocoon about the size of a large pea in which it pupates.

Ant Lion larva in pit

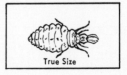

True Size

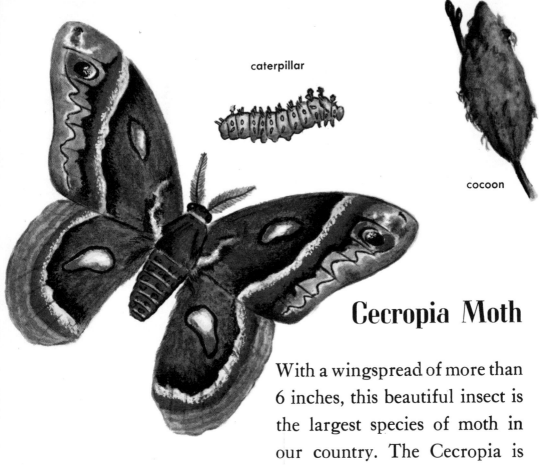

caterpillar

cocoon

Cecropia Moth

With a wingspread of more than 6 inches, this beautiful insect is the largest species of moth in our country. The Cecropia is nocturnal in habit and the adult does not require any food.

Up to 400 pinkish-white eggs are laid in rows on leaves and hatch in about 2 weeks. The larva, which is black, then red, sheds its skin several times, and when mature is green with large yellow, red, and blue tubercles.

The larva feeds on leaves of apple, maple, elm, wild cherry, willow, and many other trees and shrubs.

It then spins a cocoon which is fastened to twigs from which the adult moth emerges in late spring or summer. Some birds with beaks that are strong enough to penetrate the tough cocoons will feed upon the tasty pupa inside the cocoon.

This moth is also known by the name of Emperor Moth.

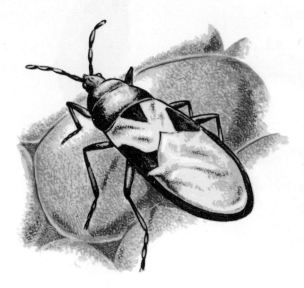

Chinch Bug

This villain is considered one of the six worst insect pests in America, and the unhappy farmer wishes it had stayed in its original home in the tropics. It makes up in numbers what it lacks in size, for it is a small fellow.

After spending the winter in corn shacks and grass tufts, Chinch Bugs fly to grain fields. Here the female lays about 500 eggs in the roots or at the base of the plants. These eggs hatch in about 2 weeks into little yellow "nymphs" that begin their destructive lives by sucking the juices of the plants, causing them to wilt and die. They spend about 40 days as "nymphs," laying waste large areas of corn fields (their favorite food) and other grain fields.

The damage caused by these pests has been known to run into millions of dollars every year. The short time spent in the nymph stage allows the Chinch Bug to develop as many as 2 or 3 generations in a single season.

Chinch Bugs seem to have found ideal living conditions in the Mississippi Valley, where they are more destructive and abundant than anywhere else.

True Size

nymph

Colorado Potato Beetle

larva

At one time this insect was quietly confining its feeding to unimportant plants in the Rocky Mountain area. It was in the year 1850, when the settlers began to grow potatoes, that this member of the Leaf Beetle family developed a brand-new taste. By 1874 it had spread eastward and had reached the Atlantic Coast, and now can be found wherever potatoes are grown except in California. It has even reached Europe.

The yellow eggs are laid on the underside of potato leaves. These hatch in about a week and the larvae which are fat, soft, and white, feed on the leaves. The larvae burrow underground, change into pupae, and then in about 2 weeks come out as adults that continue to feed on the potato plants.

True Size

Cornfield Ant

The life of ants has long been a source of interest to all and makes them favorite objects for study.

The Cornfield Ant is the most common and abundant of all our ants, and is found in fields and on lawns. The ant colony is usually established by a queen, who sheds her wings.

She lays about 200 eggs which produce workers, soldiers, males, and other queens. Once mated, the queen can produce eggs for the rest of her life, which may be as long as 10 or 15 years.

Ants keep aphids (small plant lice) for the honeydew they produce, much the same as we keep cattle. Slave ants are also used to lessen the labor of ants. These ants are seized while they are still larvae and brought home to the nests, to become servants in the colonies of the raiders.

True Size

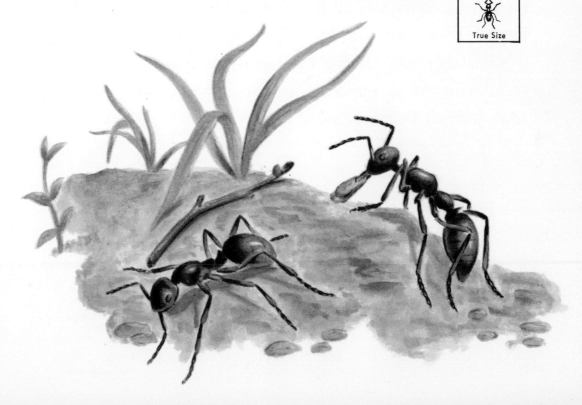

Dobson-fly

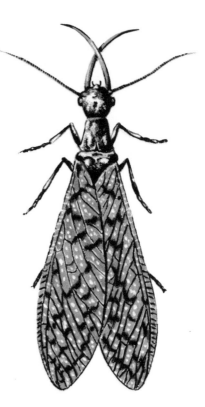

A very fierce-looking fellow is the male Dobson-fly with his long crossed jaws and a 4 to 5 inch wing-spread, but you needn't worry, he is quite harmless.

The female lays a mass of several thousand eggs on plants, stones, or other objects overhanging the water. The eggs hatch into larvae that drop into the water.

These "nymphs," or larvae, are the familiar hellgrammites that are well known to fishermen as one of the best baits for bass, trout, and perch. They live beneath stones in the shallow rapids of streams and rivers, feeding on all sorts of water insects. They can swim but usually crawl.

After about 35 months the larvae leave the water and spend a month as pupae. They then emerge and become adult winged Dobson-flies.

larva
hellgrammite

Dragon Fly

The swift-darting Dragon Fly has been falsely thought of as harmful to man, when it really is one of man's best friends in the insect world. Its food consists of the larvae of other water insects and it may eat tadpoles, but its favorites are mosquitoes and flies, and everyone knows how harmful these two can be.

We can tell the difference between the Dragon Fly and the smaller Damsel Fly, which looks very much like it, by the positions of the wings when they are at rest. The Dragon Fly holds its wings outspread, while the Damsel Fly folds its wings over its back.

Mrs. Dragon Fly places her eggs in the mud or water. In several weeks they hatch, and out come the nymphs who spend their time wandering about the bottom of a muddy pond feeding on water bugs, caddis worms, and the like.

nymph

Field Cricket

Who hasn't heard the merry chirping of a Cricket on a warm summer night? This familiar evening concert is really the love song of the male Cricket, and is accomplished by rubbing the fore wings together.

The brown or black Field Crickets are to be found everywhere in gardens, pastures, under stones, and even sometimes in dwellings. When they invade our homes, they may injure and destroy food, clothing, and the like. They are quite injurious to crops and vegetation and do most of their harmful work at night, when they are least likely to be disturbed. Though they prefer a vegetable diet, they may attack and eat other insects and also each other.

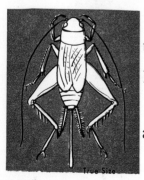

The female lays several hundred eggs in holes in the ground. The baby Cricket looks just like its parents, except it doesn't have developed wings.

You may be surprised to learn that Crickets' ears are located on their front legs.

True Size

Firefly

This is not really a fly at all, but a soft-bodied beetle. These wonderful little creatures shine like fairy lamps in the soft darkness of a summer night. There are as many as fifty different kinds of Fireflies in the United States but not all of them emit light.

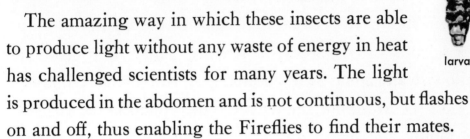

larva

The amazing way in which these insects are able to produce light without any waste of energy in heat has challenged scientists for many years. The light is produced in the abdomen and is not continuous, but flashes on and off, thus enabling the Fireflies to find their mates.

Wingless females and the larvae are called Glow Worms, and it is interesting to note that the eggs and larvae of some species will also glow. The larvae live in rubbish, rotted wood, or in the soil, feeding on other insects.

In tropical regions, a most wonderful sight is said to be the flashing, every 10 seconds, of thousands of Fireflies all at the same time.

True Size

Flies

fruit fly — ⅛"

Flies are different from most insects, since they seem to be able to fly as well with a single pair of wings as other insects can with two pairs.

Some flies are scavengers and others are effective controls on some harmful insects.

Fruit flies have become important in the laboratories of our scientists in the study of heredity. These little flies are yellowish and about ⅛ of an inch long with bright red eyes.

Like the Mosquito, the female is the villain in the Horse-fly family and few if any animals can outrace this swift-flying pest.

The fisherman or camper is familiar with the pesky Deer Fly that buzzes around his head and also around the ears of horses.

The Robber Fly never attacks man or animal and may be seen preying upon other flies, butterflies, beetles, and moths.

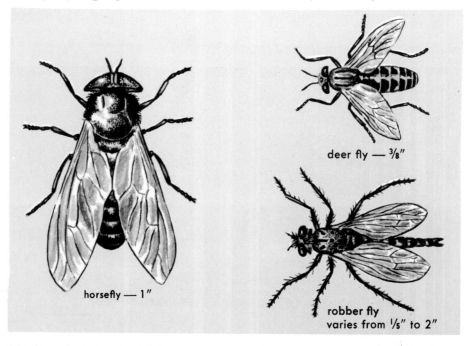

horsefly — 1"

deer fly — ⅜"

robber fly
varies from ⅕" to 2"

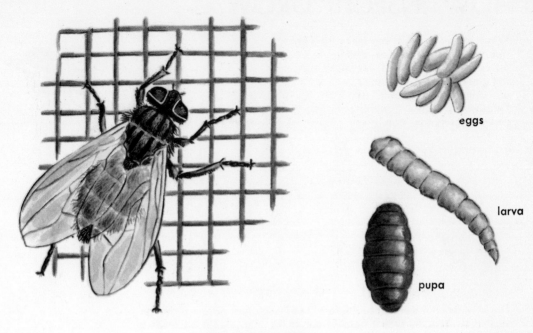

eggs

larva

pupa

House Fly

This is the true villain of the insect world and should be swatted or avoided, whichever is more effective at the moment. Flies are said to be capable of spreading 30 to 40 different diseases. The germs are carried on the hairs of the legs or are swallowed and vomited out again.

Up to 600 eggs are laid in clusters, usually in manure exposed to sunshine. These hatch in a very short time—in warm weather in about 10 hours, or 3 days in cool weather. Larvae are called maggots. These become fully developed in about 5 days; then they pupate for about 5 more days and emerge as full-grown adults.

The time from the egg to the adult fly is about 2 weeks. There are about a dozen generations a year, so you can see that it is possible for one female in April to have 5½ trillion descendants by September.

True Size

HOW INSECTS GROW

When insects grow, many times they go through different stages during which they hardly look at all like what they will grow up to be. This series of changes is known as "metamorphosis," which means "change in form."

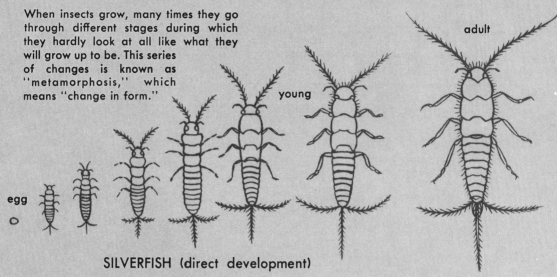

SILVERFISH (direct development)

The Silverfish is a member of the family of insects that does not change very much from the time it hatches out of the egg, until it becomes a full-grown adult. This development is known as direct and there is no "metamorphosis."

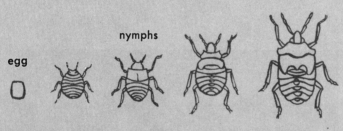
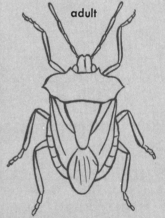

BUG (simple development)

Another form of growth is that which is shown above and is known as "simple development" (incomplete metamorphosis). The bug, when it hatches is not entirely different than its parents. At first it doesn't have wings, but these grow slowly as the bug grows. The young of insects which develop this way are called "nymphs," and they must shed their skins several times before they will become adults.

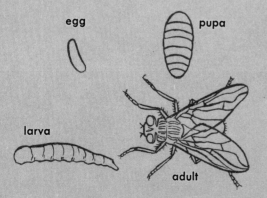

FLY (complex development)

The most advanced type of growth is shown using the fly as an example. This is called "complete metamorphosis" and consists of four stages. (1) the egg; (2) the larva, which hatches from the egg and gradually grows larger, shedding its skin as it grows; the larva of the moth and butterfly is the familiar caterpillar; (3) the pupa, in which the wonderful change takes place and the larva becomes the adult insect, which resembles neither the pupa nor the larva. Another form of pupa is the cocoon. The pupa of the butterfly is called a chrysalis.

Giant Water Bug

This very large bug, 2 to 4 inches long, is also known as the Electric Light Bug, because it is attracted by strong lights and sometimes gathers in large numbers around them.

The powerful forelegs are used to capture other water insects, frogs, and small fish. These bugs have been known to kill fish four times their own size, and may invade fish hatcheries, where they destroy eggs, young, and even the adult fish.

Eggs of the Giant Water Bug hatch in 1 to 2 weeks, the young being little copies of the parents, with the exception of the wing development. They go through 5 stages of growth before they mature.

The Smaller Giant Water Bug, a close relative, resembles the one pictured in everything but size. The female of this species fastens the fertilized eggs to the back of the male, where he carries them until they hatch.

Harlequin Stinkbug

Don't let its gay coat fool you, for the Harlequin Stinkbug is no clown or laughing matter. Considered by many to be one of our worst pests, it does, however, have its interesting side. Its eggs, which number an even dozen, are neatly arranged, and look very much like tiny white decorated beer barrels, 6 in a row.

It is believed that the disagreeable odor that this and other members of the Stinkbug family give off is a means of discouraging birds and other enemies from eating them.

Our farmers in the South have a special dislike for this insect, for that is where it does the most damage. It can be found hard at work destroying such crops as cabbages, turnips, and radishes, among many others. It is so fond of cabbage that it is often called the Harlequin Cabbage Bug.

True Size

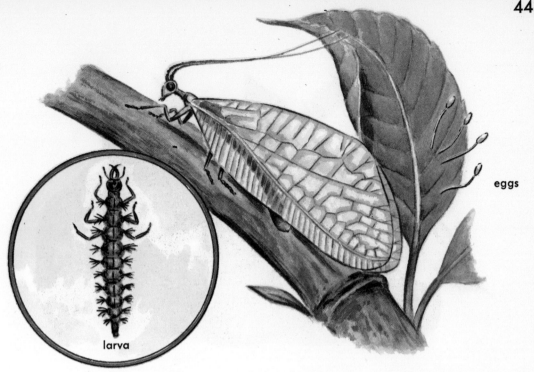

eggs

larva

Green Lacewing

The delicate green Lacewing, sometimes known as Golden-eye, is to be found on plants in our orchards and gardens. Often called "Greenflies," although not true flies, both the adult Lacewings and larvae will eat large quantities of aphids. Because the larvae feed on aphids so heartily they are called aphid-lions. Aphids are small, harmful plant insects.

The mother Lacewing has a most interesting manner of laying her eggs. The tip of her abdomen touches a leaf or twig and releases a small amount of fluid. Then she lifts her abdomen and the fluid is drawn out like a thread and an egg is laid on the end.

This method of laying eggs is used for a good reason. When they hatch, the larvae are so hungry that the first one out would eat up all the rest if they weren't protected by stalks of their own.

True Size

Japanese Beetle

A very undesirable immigrant, this shiny green Beetle was accidentally introduced into this country in 1916 from Japan and is quite a serious pest now. Some natural enemies of this insect have been imported from Japan in an effort to control the Japanese Beetle.

The food of this beetle and its larvae is many kinds of cultivated trees and shrubs, such as grapes, strawberries, blackberries, apples, cherries, and corn, as well as roses and other valuable plants.

Tiny white eggs are laid in the ground sometime in the month of July. The larvae, which are white, hatch from these eggs, and spend the summer feeding. They hibernate during the winter, enter the pupal stage during the spring, and emerge as adults in June or July.

True Size

Katydid

Have you ever wondered what it was that made the familiar sound, "Katy did, Katy she did, she did," on a summer night or on a cloudy day? If you look closely in the daytime, you might find this little green grasshopper. Its coloring, which is so much like the leaves it sits on, helps to hide it from its enemies. This is called protective coloration.

Some Katydids live in trees and feed on the leaves while others seem to prefer to spend their time in the grass, tall weeds, or bushes during the day.

The song we spoke of before is made by Mr. Katydid rubbing the bases of his wing covers together, much like a person playing on a fiddle.

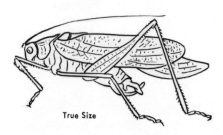

Eggs are laid in the fall and the young are born the following spring. They look very much like their parents but lack wings, which develop later as they grow. There is no pupal stage.

True Size

Ladybird Beetle

This is among the most useful of all insects and should be treated like the good friend of man that it is. Ladybird Beetles are usually red, black, or yellow, and spotted with white, red, yellow, or black.

pupa

They feed on aphids (plant lice) and the eggs of some very harmful insects, such as the Chinch Bug, Colorado Potato Beetle, and many others. When an Australian insect pest was ruining the fruit trees in California, an Australian Ladybird Beetle was imported and in a short time the pest was completely wiped out.

Eggs are laid in the spring. The larvae eat insect eggs and small insects. The mature larvae then becomes a pupa, and hangs head down for a few days before becoming an adult.

larva

True Size

Luna Moth

Also known as the "Pale Empress of the Night," this beautiful moth is a favorite of amateur collectors.

The Luna as well as the Cecropia is a member of the Giant Silkworm family, whose bodies are comparatively heavy and covered with hair and whose wings are wide and strong.

The white eggs, as many as 200, are fastened to twigs and upper leaf surfaces, hatch in about 3 weeks, and come out clear green caterpillars. After shedding 4 times, and about a month from the time it hatched, the larva or caterpillar spins a thin, leaf-covered cocoon in which the pupa will spend the winter.

Food of the Luna Moth larva consists of the leaves of the walnut, hickory, sweet gum, and many other trees.

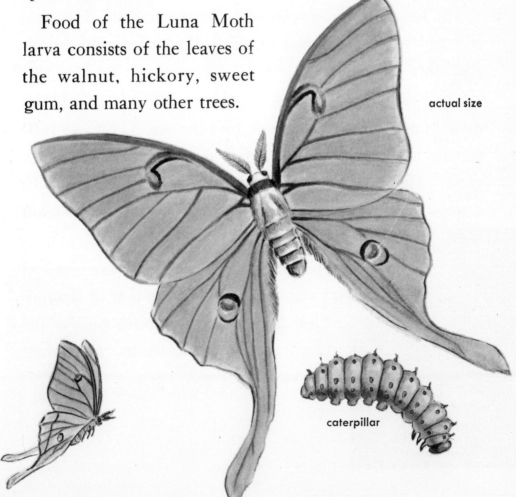

actual size

caterpillar

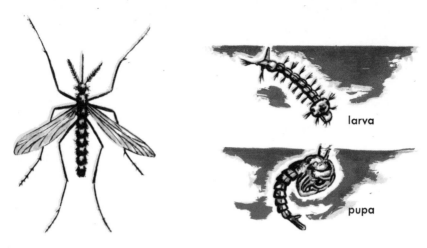

larva

pupa

Mosquitoes

Mosquitoes are known for their disease-carrying abilities. In tropic areas the Malaria Mosquito is responsible for spreading Malaria.

The female of the species is the dangerous one. The male is harmless and is content to satisfy his hunger with nectar and other plant juices.

The eggs of the mosquito are laid in rafts of several hundred, in ponds, ditches, barrels, tin cans, etc. These egg rafts usually hatch in from 1 to 5 days into larvae called "wrigglers." They feed on very small animal life in the water. In a week or two they become pupae and in 4 or 5 days adult mosquitoes.

The mosquito has many natural enemies and forms an important part of the diet of dragonflies, damsel flies, and birds such as flycatchers, swallows, swifts, and night hawks.

malaria mosquito

house mosquito

True Size

Praying Mantis

A welcome guest in our gardens is the Praying
Mantis, for it destroys many harmful pests.

egg case

Although it can fly, it prefers to wait on a tree
or shrub until an unsuspecting insect comes by.
As soon as the Mantis sees its intended dinner, it moves
quietly and carefully toward it. Then suddenly, like a flash
of lightning, the forelegs shoot out and the victim is caught.

The female lays small groups of eggs that are surrounded
by a protective covering. These are attached to a board,
twigs, or even a building. They hatch in May or June into
tiny Mantes that look just like their parents, lacking only
the wings. A male Mantis is liable to be eaten by his mate
if he is not careful.

A Mantis kept in a glass tank makes an interesting pet, if you are willing to supply it with
live insects.

Tiger Beetle

This brightly colored, metallic green beetle with its long thin legs is probably not too often seen at close range because it is rather difficult to capture.

larva

Tiger Beetles are to be found on the shores of streams, woodland trails, and on hot days on dusty roads. At night, they retire to holes in the ground or under stones.

The eggs are laid singly in the soil, and the larvae are just as fierce but not so pretty as their parents. They are sometimes known as "Doodlebugs." They dig deep burrows, then wait at the top to catch any careless insect that might pass by. They are even equipped with hooks on their backs which prevent them from being pulled out of their burrows by a stronger insect. The larvae will seal off the entrance hole and pupate in the burrow.

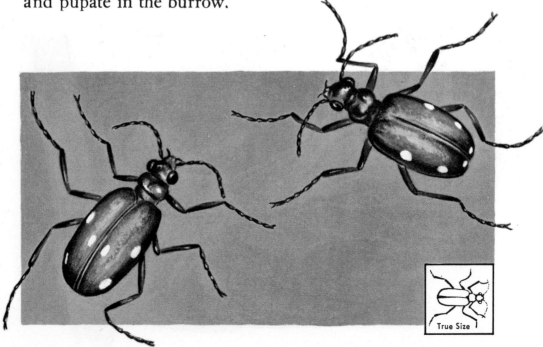

True Size

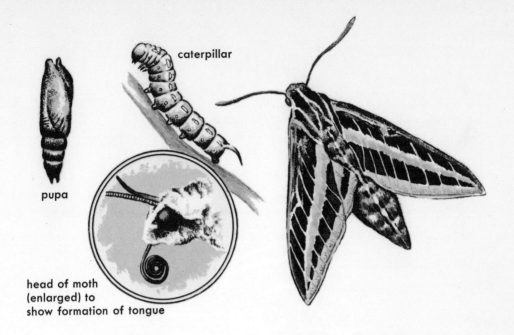

caterpillar

pupa

head of moth
(enlarged) to
show formation of tongue

White-Lined Sphinx Moth

There are about one hundred species of Sphinx Moths in this country. They are very often mistaken for hummingbirds because of their large size (5-inch wingspread) and their habit of hovering over flowers with wings beating so rapidly as to be invisible.

This moth is equipped with a marvelous tongue, which is really a sucking tube, and when not in use is coiled up underneath the head like a watch spring. This long tongue enables the moth to obtain nectar and pollinate such flowers as petunias, honeysuckle, and other tubular flowers.

The larvae, which hatch from large, shiny green eggs, are green, have a horn on the tail, and are therefore sometimes known as Hornworms.

The larvae spend 4 weeks as caterpillars, then pupate in the soil or among rubbish and leaves on the ground.

Sphinx with wings spread